ALSO BY ROBERT FULGHUM

All I Really Need to Know
I Learned in Kindergarten

It Was on Fire When I Lay Down on It

All I Really Need to Know
I Learned in Kindergarten
(gift edition)

Happy '91 Birthday
Vince
15th of September

Uh-Oh

Uh-Oh

Robert Fulghum

Published by Random House Large Print
in association with Villard Books

New York 1991

A brief portion of this book appeared in slightly
different form in *Newsweek.*

Library of Congress Cataloging-in-Publication Data
Fulghum, Robert.
Uh-Oh
Robert Fulghum —Large print ed.
p. cm.
ISBN 0-679-40286-1 (lg. print)
1. Life. 2. Large type books. I. Title
[BD431.F87 1991b]
814'.54—dc20   90-50926

9 8 7 6 5 4 3 2
First Large Print Edition

THIS LARGE PRINT BOOK CARRIES
THE SEAL OF APPROVAL OF N.A.V.H.

Uh-Oh

"Uh-oh" is not in any dictionary or thesaurus, and is seldom seen in written form. Yet most of us utter that sound every day. And have used it all our lives.

"Uh-oh" is one of the first expressions a baby learns.

"Uh-oh," or something like it, has been used as long as people have existed. And it may be the first thing Adam said to Eve after he bit into the apple.

She knew exactly what he meant, too.

Across the history of the human family, millions and millions of distinct sounds have come and gone as we continually reach for ways to communicate with one another. Often, the most expressive words we use are not words at all, just those shorthand sounds that represent complex thoughts—grunts and moans and snorts and clicks and whistles compounded by facial expressions and physical gestures: "Uh-huh . . . no-no . . . mmmnnn . . . huh . . . hey . . . oops . . . OK . . . yo . . . ah . . . ha . . . humpf . . . and an almost endless number of others whose meaning and spelling cannot be conveyed with letters on paper.

"Uh-oh" is way up near the top of a list of small syllables with large meanings.

We say "uh-oh" to a small child who falls down or bumps his head or pinches his finger. It means that we know the child hurts, but we also know the hurt is temporary and that the child has the resources to handle the hurt and get up and go on about his business. As the child learns, he will not need to turn to a parent to kiss-it-and-make-it-well each time he scrapes himself—he will know where to find the bandages on his own. "Uh-oh" is the first wedge in weaning a child away from us into independence.

The older we get, the more experience and knowledge we have, the more able we are to distinguish momentary difficulty from serious trouble. The more we know that something is "uh-oh," not 911.

If I had a chest pain, I might go to an emergency room thinking "Oh my God, heart attack!" If my doctor had the same symptoms, she might think, Uh-oh, gas pains, take an antacid, and go on with her work.

What to me is the last gasp of my old truck is a repairable electric problem to my mechanic. "Uh-oh, there's a short in your ignition wire."

One might even come to feel the same way about things that cannot be fixed. From the cradle we know about "Rock-a-bye-baby" and what happens when the bough breaks. In kindergarten we are reminded about these conditions. All the king's horses and all the king's men could not put Humpty Dumpty together again. I'm familiar with death, having been around it often in hospitals and cemeteries. If I see my own death coming, my response may well be "uh-oh."

"Uh-oh" in this sense is a frame of mind. A philosophy.

It says to expect the unexpected, and also expect to be able to deal with it as it happens most of the time. "Uh-oh" people seem not only to expect surprise, but they count on it, as if surprise were a dimension of vitality.

"Uh-oh" embraces "Here we go again" and "Now what?" and "You never can tell what's going to happen next" and "So much for plan

A" and "Hang on, we're coming to a tunnel" and "No sweat" and "Tomorrow's another day" and "You can't unscramble an egg" and "A hundred years from now it won't make any difference."

"Uh-oh" is more than a momentary reaction to small problems. "Uh-oh" is an attitude—a perspective on the universe. It is part of an equation that summarizes my view of the conditions of existence:

$$\text{"uh-huh"} + \text{"oh-wow"} + \text{"uh-oh"} + \text{"oh, God"} = \text{"ah-hah!"}$$

"*H*um a little something for me."

"Why?"

"So I can tell you what key your head is in."

"I don't understand."

"Your head is a sound chamber, and every sound chamber resonates to certain notes better than others because of the shape and size and construction of the chamber."

I am a visitor in a high school science class, and the teacher is using me to demonstrate to his class that adults don't know everything. All his students already know what their key is and how and why. I don't. So he sends me off to do some personal research in a small, empty room. To hum and haw until I sound a note I really like—one that makes my head vibrate a little—in a comfortable and pleasing way. Easy. It's like standing in the shower singing, with my clothes on and the water off.

When the note felt right, I reported back to the classroom, where the science wizard put me in front of a microphone and said, "Hum for me." I hummed. The oscilloscope reflected the wave structure of my voice.

"B-flat," he announced. "Fulghum, you have a head that's tuned in the key of B-flat major—which is a sixty-cycle tone with natural overtones of D and F, forming the triadic complex of the chord."

Later I learned that trumpets and clarinets are also B-flat instruments, which means a lot of good jazz is in B-flat. Fanfares and marching-band music are often written in B-flat, which makes it the key of parades and spectacles. At the racetrack, the trumpet call announcing each race is in B-flat. "The Star-Spangled Banner" and the "Marseillaise" are in the same key. And the "William Tell Overture" should be.

And my refrigerator hums in B-flat major.

The electric motor of the refrigerator gives off a sixty-cycle B-flat hum, as do all motors that run on 120-volt AC current. The washing machine, dryer, electric heater, blender, hair dryer, coffeepot, and all the rest are B-flat appliances. What's more, even when no motors are running, there is a sixty-cycle leak of energy from all the wall sockets in the house. My house is immersed in B-flat, which may explain why a man with a B-flat head like me really feels at home there. And also may explain why I feel so good near the refrigerator. I am in harmony with it. Now I know why I sometimes sing the national anthem when I invade the refrigerator in the middle of the night.

Refrigerators. On a very local scale, a refrigerator is the center of the universe. On the inside is food essential to life, and on the outside of the door is a summary of the life events of the household. Grocery lists, report cards, gems of wisdom, cartoons, family schedules, urgent bills, reminders, instructions, complaints, photographs, postcards, lost and found items, and commands. When the word *GARBAGE* appears there, somebody had better move it and soon.

The door of the refrigerator is a chronicle of current events not found on TV or in the daily newspaper.

An important art gallery is often found here as well. Postcards of paintings from museums.

Scribbles from a child's long, rainy afternoon with a box of crayons. A collection of drawings, collages, and paintings that come home from school in a steady stream. All stuck to the front of the family fridge.

When you no longer have any art on the refrigerator door, something is over—your children have grown up. And when it appears again years later, it means your children have children. Grandparents are suckers for refrigerator art and will put up just about anything offered them by a child of their child.

I'd like to sponsor a national contest to see who has the most amazing collection of stuff on their fridge—and produce a book of photographs of refrigerator decor. Each photograph would be accompanied by a page of explanation, including a list of all items contained inside and on top of the refrigerator as well. This could be the coffee-table book of the year.

"But my refrigerator has nothing on it—what does that say about me?" you may ask.

It means you are a nice person who has carried neatness in the kitchen one step further than the *Good Housekeeping* Seal of Approval requires. Lighten up. Get some magnets—the heavy-duty kind—and get your stuff up on the door of the fridge. If you aren't sure about what to put there, consult with friends.

Many people know about what should go on the fridge door and will be glad to advise you.

Ever been present at one of those archeological expeditions when the entire contents of the refrigerator, freezer included, are laid out on the kitchen counters?

How can people *live* like this?

From the freezer compartment come especially interesting bits of history. Like a package of mystery meat with freezer burn so bad you don't know whether to bandage it, smoke it, or use it to start a fire. I recall discovering such things as a snowball, the corpse of a very small shrew, some ice cream made from snow, a corsage from a wedding anniversary, and several flashlight batteries—all frozen into the last ice age of the freezing compartment of our refrigerator. All placed in safekeeping in the deep cold by various members of the family for their own reasons. All important to the persons who put them there. What should be done with these relics? I ran across an idea from the National Park Service that has merit. It asks that any historical artifacts found in a park be appreciated by the finder, left in place, and simply reported to headquarters so that experts may deal with removal or disposal. From hard experience, I urge that those who clean out freezers at home follow the Park Service policy. Those who reclaim their treasures will love you more if they don't have to exhume half-thawed relics from the garbage can.

Unless you are happily sound asleep at that hour, 2:00 A.M. is usually not the best of times. It's an hour often given to pacing the floor in crisis or in grief—or to consoling of wee babes who cry in the night. Telephones that ring at 2:00 A.M. usually mean trouble, as do sounds made by teenagers arriving home late, disturbed dogs, dripping water, and those unknown creatures that gnaw somewhere in the walls. People talk to themselves about serious things at this hour.

I think of 2:00 A.M. as feeding time. The time when I've had some of the best meals I've ever eaten. Gourmet eating. Alone. With nobody standing around saying, "You're not really going to *eat* THAT, are you?"

One memorable midnight I put away a taco shell full of almond paste and washed it down with a can of Snap-e-Tom that had been there so long there was rust on the can. Followed that with some celery sticks limp enough to tie granny knots in. Then I ate a whole dish of tapioca pudding that I picked up out of the bowl in one piece. The last inch from a bottle of red wine made way for a scoop of cold chili smeared on rye bread and topped with fig jam. A spoonful of peanut butter and a spoonful of jam every now and then to clear the palate. A couple of glasses of milk to keep things moving on down my throat without jamming up. Finally, I revived a cup of dead coffee in the microwave and went out on the porch to sit and look at the moon and smoke the remaining half of a cigar I hadn't finished before I went up to bed a couple of nights before. Great meal. One of the *truly* great ones.

Another dead-of-the-night dining extravaganza happened because I sat up late reading *The White Trash Cookbook.* There's a recipe in there for "Rack of Spam." You take a can of Spam, which we just happened to have—left over from a camping trip—and you butterfly the loaf, which means slicing it in thin sections without cutting all the way through. Then you bend the Spam open so you can stick pieces of pineapple in between them. (That's what that half a can of hairy pineapple chunks on the back shelf of the refrigerator is meant for.) For garnish, top off with some peanut butter and a few maraschino cherries. Stick that baby in the microwave for about four minutes.

Open a box of saltine crackers and get a whole quart of milk from the fridge—drink it right from the carton. Take your time and eat it all.

You can't get a meal like this in a French restaurant, but I've seldom eaten better.

The recipes in the cookbooks and the meals we really eat are not the same thing.

Just as a map and the highway it describes are not the same thing.

The map does not tell of sun, roadwork, grumpy companions, or the games played with children in a car. And the cookbook does not speak of the pleasures of winging it alone in the kitchen in the dead of night, eating without rules.

Maps and cookbooks help—they are one way of describing reality.

Manuals have their uses . . . but they are not to be confused with the living.

What I really look forward to finding in the fridge in a time of late-night need is meatloaf. Now we're getting serious. Meatloaf.

When I say those words, people usually smile. And then I ask, "Why are you smiling?" And then they laugh. "Why are you laughing?" And they laugh again. "Meatloaf—haw, haw,

haw—meatloaf—haw, haw, haw." One of the many mysterious powers of meatloaf.

Mom's Cafe at the four-way stop in Salina, Utah, is high on my list of great places to eat. Mom's advertises THE BEST IN HOMEMADE PIES, SCONES, SOUP, AND MUCH, MUCH MORE!! Mom's specializes in liver and onions, chicken-fried steak, deep-fried chicken, "real" french fries, and "real" mashed potatoes. But Mom's doesn't serve meatloaf. I called them long-distance to check my facts. The lady who answered the phone was a little surprised that I asked. "Don't you know nothing? Meatloaf is something you eat at home."

It's true. Meatloaf is mostly homemade. Mostly made by real moms, by hand. Constructed out of what's around. Some hamburger that might be going bad if it isn't used soon—sprouting potatoes, rubbery carrots, onions, salt, pepper, steak sauce, bacon drippings, etcetera. I say "etcetera" because the list of what's possible is too long to print. Then there's the filler—meatloaf expander. Bread crumbs, corn flakes, Rice Crispies, oatmeal, or whatever—even dirt would work, I guess. And some egg to hold the whole thing together. Then it has to be mushed around by hand, kneaded into a loaf, and put into that family museum piece the meatloaf pan. Into the oven to bake. Served hot with gravy, mashed potatoes, and Wonder bread. Yes. Yes!

But don't eat it all. Never ever eat all the meatloaf when it's fresh. Put about a third of it away in the back of the fridge and forget about it. This is the best part. The part you are going to eat about 2:00 A.M. some dark, rainy night when you need sustaining. No health department would allow such a thing to be served in a public restaurant. But nothing's better for you. It's a matter of mental health. I've never heard anybody say he was depressed by eating a cold meatloaf sandwich.

I'm a mayonnaise-and-sourdough-bread man, myself. I know there are ketchup people and mustard people and even jelly people. A kid once joined me in this middle-of-the-night feasting, and I made him very happy by fixing him a meatloaf sandwich with Gummi Bears, grape jam, and Fritos on it. It's a free country.

Now I now that some people don't like meat-loaf. This is true. At a summer camp a group of children complained to me that the adults all gathered around the campfire and sang pro-test songs (the sixties ones) against war and hate and all that, which was fine with the kids, but they would like it if we sang a children's protest song or two. Like what? Well, they couldn't think of one offhand, but they were pretty unhappy about the meatloaf served in the mess hall two nights in a row. So we made up the Meatloaf Protest Song.

"Eat your meatloaf," whined the
mommy at the table.
"Eat your meatloaf or your teeth will all
fall out!"
"Eat your meatloaf," whined the
mommy at the table.
In reply, all the little children shout:

Chorus:
"We don't want to eat the meatloaf!
Meatloaf is fit for pigs and goats.
Red and yellow, black and white, it is
icky in our sight!
You can't make us shove that nasty
down our throats!"

(For "meatloaf" you can substitute other items of food deemed deadly by children: liver, lima beans, tofu, whatever. It's hard to convey the tune here, but the chorus sounds a lot like "Jesus Loves the Little Children." But, like meatloaf itself, whatever tune you come up with that works for you is OK. Try it on your kids. Be prepared for many verses.)

...

Meatloaf reminds me of other brands of leftovers. Especially Thanksgiving leftovers. When the refrigerator becomes the Fort Knox of late-night dining. Let's face it, Thanksgiving is often a strain. You have to dress up and behave and there's all that ritual fuss and bother with too many people and too much food. Exhausting. But two nights later is a different story. There's good news in the fridge by then—solid-gold leftovers.

The pecan pie has ripened and congealed now, so you can pick up a big piece with your hand. The cranberry sauce has matured; the dark meat of the turkey is easy to peel off the bone. And the dressing has transmogrified into something that would give truffles and caviar a run for the money. THIS is the way dressing ought to taste! A true prayer of thanksgiving is in order.

This is not a group activity. It is a private religious experience. In the holy solitude of the midnight hour, you are taking communion with the spirits of bird and fruit and field. The best moments of past feasts come to mind. And it is at times like these you have no doubt that life is good, that your family, all tucked away in their beds, are royal folks, and that grace abounds. Amen.

. . .

Leftovers in their less visible form are called memories.

Stored in the refrigerator of the mind and the cupboard of the heart.

These are just a few of mine that came up tonight: the laughter of a friend, the last embers of a great fire, the long glance of love from my spouse from across a room full of people, an unexpected snowfall, the year everything went wrong and turned out right, and a chunk of poetry I learned in high school.

I'm not often aware that I am happy. But I often remember that I have been happy. Especially when I sit in my kitchen wrapped in an invisible patchwork quilt made of the best moments of yesterdays.

These precious things—these leftovers from living on—remain to serve as survival rations for the heart and soul. You can't entirely live off them. But life is not worth living without them.

My solitary late-night forays for food in the fridge are often garnished with such thoughts.

I don't go to the refrigerator just to eat. But to think. To sort it all out. And sometimes I think about the other people who must be at the same place in their kitchen at this very moment, doing exactly what I'm doing, hungering as I hunger, wondering as I wonder. We will never get together. There will never be an international convention of us. No kitchen is big enough. But we are bound together. We make up that secret society of the Fellowship of the Fridge. Somehow muddling through and getting by. And not really as alone as we often think we are, after all.

*T*his book has a Hudson's Bay Start.

In the glory days of fur trading in North America during the eighteenth century, the Hudson's Bay Company was known for both its willingness to take adventuresome risks and its careful preparation for those risks. Trading journeys were habitually begun with vigorous enthusiasm, yet the frontiersmen always camped the first night a few short miles from the company headquarters. This allowed the gear and supplies to be sorted and considered, so that if anything had been left behind in the haste to be under way, it was easy to return to the post to fetch it. A meeting was held with all participants to make sure they understood the nature and details of the expedition. A thoughtful beginning spared the travelers later difficulties.

I learned about the Hudson's Bay Start when I began backpacking in high school years. It seemed such a sensible thing to do. To this day, I still make it a dimension of almost any trip. Cover a few easy miles the first day, check equipment, review maps, make sure I'm in sync with my companions, relax, eat a fine meal, go to bed early, and sleep well. The next day is usually a fine one, setting the tone for the rest of the way.

In that Hudson's Bay tradition, I want to pause here not far from the beginning of this book, to speak of the two-person experience undertaken between reader and writer.

First, I'll acknowledge that I am well aware of the canon of literary law that says a writer is not supposed to write in his book about the process of writing his book. "Show them, don't tell them; do it, don't talk about doing it" is an admonition hammered home by every good editor and teacher of writing. On the other hand, speechwriters are told the contrary: "Tell them what you're going to tell them; tell them; and tell them what you told them."

I believe in both Show *and* Tell. My attitude is that I am always talking to one person, and

if I am going to address you in any form, I
ought to give you every advantage I can to
understand what I have to say. This emphati-
cally does not mean that I underestimate your
intelligence. It means that I am aware how
complicated communication is. It means that I
would rather err on the side of telling you too
much than run the risk of leaving you confused. It means I have a profound respect for
our differences and will try to bridge them
wherever and however I can.

I admit there is a division of opinion over this
matter. There are those who do not like to
read reviews of books and movies before-
hand; those who don't want to read program
notes at concerts, and those who do not like
to know what the authors or actors or directors
think about their own work before experienc-
ing a performance. My wife is one of these. I
am not. But we honor our differences.

I don't know what your opinion is in this matter, so as a gesture of good faith, I offer you
a choice here. The Hudson's Bay Start may
not be your style. If you'd like to plunge on into
the rest of the book, please do. Just skip over
now to page 37. If you'd like to know now what
I have to say about the way this particular book
is put together, read on.

. . .

I'm writing this time in what I think of as "lines-of-thought." Much as conversation is carried on between two people. One thing leads to another, there's a pausing now and then, and the end of a conversation isn't always directly connected to the beginning. Nothing definitive is intended on any subject. In fact, I am deliberately depending on your adding your thoughts and experiences to mine as we go— to give completion to our conversation. The book will not work without your taking significant responsibility for it.

My own movement of thought is not meant to be a straight point-to-point, linear line of march, but a horizontal exploration from one area of interest to another. There is no ultimate destination—no finish line to cross, no final conclusion to be reached. It's the way I feel about dancing—you move around a lot, not to get somewhere, but to be somewhere in time.

Two visual artists have significantly affected my thinking about writing: Paul Cézanne and Constantin Brancusi. Cézanne painted the same mountain in Provence over and over again. He was not interested as much in Mont-Sainte-Victoire as he was in the play of light and shadow and color on the mountain. His painting was always about the essence of a thing and not the thing itself. Brancusi's subject matter also may seem limited. By the time Brancusi died in 1957, he had made many versions of a few ideas. One major work, "Bird in Space," was carried to completion at least twenty-eight times, in wood, marble, plaster, and bronze. Each version was slightly different. Each time he was trying to express his feeling about flying. He wanted to catch an idea in the air—soaring itself. He succeeded. Almost every survey of art history in print has a photograph of one of Brancusi's birds. As do the major modern-art museums of the world.

It's true he was hammered by the critics in his own day for not turning out a wider variety of subject matter—for working away at the same themes over and over instead of moving on to do new things.

Brancusi explained that innovation was not his way. Only a few very basic subjects engaged him—very common aspects of existence: a kiss, the beginning of life, the Prodigal Son, human beauty—and he wanted to keep trying to cut away everything extraneous to his feelings about these subjects and express them as simply as possible in sculpture.

As you've read along in this book so far—and especially if you've already read my two previous books—you will notice that I have come back again and again to a few themes that hold my concern fast. Questions, actually, that I keep on the front burner of my mental stove. Such as:

How shall I achieve a living balance be-
     tween the mundane and the holy?
Between humor and grief?
Between what is and what might be?
Between self-concern and concern for
     the common good?
Between the worst that I often am and the
     best I might well become?
And is it really possible to do unto others
     as I'd have them do unto me, and why
     is it so damn hard?

If you notice phrases, ideas, and anecdotes that closely resemble those that appear else-where in my writing, it is not a matter of sloppy editing. I'm repeating myself. I'm reshuffling words in the hope that just once I might say something exactly right. And I'm still wrestling with dilemmas that are not easily resolved or easily dismissed. I run at them again and again because I am not finished with them. And may never be. Work-in-progress on a life-in-prog-ress is what my writing is about. And some progress in the work is enough to keep it going on.

This attitude is inspired by the man who invented the essay form.

Michel Eyquem de Montaigne. During his life he was known as a lawyer, scholar, traveler, diplomat, politician, thinker, and writer. His resources for writing were sixteenth-century France, his experiences as a member of the court of Henry III, and his term as mayor of Bordeaux. His best resource was his own daily life. His reputation today rests largely on the strength of his autobiography, *Les Essais de Michel Seigneur de Montaigne*—the *Essays* of Montaigne. The candid informality of this unique journal has led me to think of Montaigne as a friend and mentor.

He coined the word *"essai"* from the French verb *"essayer"*—to try—in the sense of testing thought and experience for merit. Montaigne meant to sort through his life as truthfully as possible. And to *try* to understand himself and his world as he went along, without coming to any final conclusions. He focused on means, not ends. *"Mon métier et mon art c'est vivre,"* he wrote. My trade and my art is living.

True to his word, he deemed no subject

beyond consideration. Philosophy, farting, war-horses, politics, sleep, religion, sneezing, conscience, rare meat, virtue, kidney stones, vanity, imaginary enemas, radishes, justice, and the relationship between father and sons—these are just a few of the thousands of topics he addressed.

It is remarkable that he did not write defensively or in a pontifical manner. His essays retain that quality of comfortable confidentiality that marks the conversations of close companions.

It is even more noteworthy that Montaigne insisted that his ideas and concerns were not original.

Commenting on his essays, he wrote: "It might well be said of me that here I have merely made up a bunch of other men's flowers, and have brought nothing of my own but the string that ties them together in a bunch, which I gladly offer to you."

If that is the case, I appreciate the care with which he chose his string.

I think Mike Montaigne is a member of the Fellowship of the Fridge. I imagine he'd like some slices of aged pâté on country bread with a little Dijon mustard and some pickles; on the side, the remains of a bowl of sweet pudding. With a glass of red *vin ordinaire.* It may sound like gourmet French cuisine, but it's really meatloaf and leftovers.

As the final item of this Hudson's Bay Start, a comment about pace in setting out from here. I realize that it's my part to write this book and your part to read it; and since you don't tell me how to write it, I shouldn't tell you how to read it. But it may help to emphasize that it was written one part at a time, and the odds are that it will make more sense if it's read the same way.

A kindergarten teacher I know was asked to have her class dramatize a fairy tale for a teacher's conference. After much discussion, the children achieved consensus on that old favorite, "Cinderella." The classic old "rags to riches" story that never dies. "Cream will rise" is the moral of this tale—someday you may get what you think you deserve. It's why adults play the lottery with such passion.

"Cinderella" was a good choice from the teacher's point of view because there were many parts and lots of room for discretionary padding of parts so that every child in the class could be in the play. A list of characters was compiled as the class talked through the plot

of the drama: There was the absolutely ravish-
ing Cinderella, the evil stepmother, the two
wicked and dumb stepsisters, the beautiful
and wise fairy godmother, the pumpkin, mice,
coachman, horses, the king, all the people at
the king's ball—generals, admirals, knights,
princesses, and, of course, that ultimate object of fabled desire, the Prince—good news
incarnate.

The children were allowed to choose roles
for themselves. As the parts were allotted,
each child was labeled with felt pen and paper,
and sent to stand over on the other side of the
room while casting was completed. Finally,
every child had a part.

Except one.

One small boy. Who had remained quiet and
disengaged from the selection process. A
somewhat enigmatic kid—"different"—and
because he was plump for his age, often
teased by the other children.

"Well, Norman," said the teacher, "who are
you going to be?"

"Well," replied Norman, "I am going to be
the pig."

"Pig? There's no pig in this story."

"Well, there is now."

Wisdom was fortunately included in the
teacher's tool bag. She looked carefully at

Norman. What harm? It was a bit of casting to type. Norman did have a certain pigginess about him, all right. So be it. Norman was declared the pig in the story of Cinderella. Nobody else wanted to be the pig, anyhow, so it was quite fine with the class. And since there was nothing in the script explaining what the pig was supposed to do, the action was left up to Norman.

As it turned out, Norman gave himself a walk-on part. The pig walked along with Cinderella wherever Cinderella went, ambling along on all fours in a piggy way, in a costume of his own devising—pink long underwear complete with trapdoor rear flap, pipe-cleaner tail, and a paper cup for a nose. He made no sound. He simply sat on his back haunches and observed what was going on, like some silently supportive Greek chorus. The expressions on his face reflected the details of the dramatic action. Looking worried, sad, anxious, hopeful, puzzled, mad, bored, sick, and pleased as the moment required. There was no doubt about what was going on, and no doubt that it was important. One look at the pig and you knew. The pig was so earnest. So sincere. So very "there." The pig brought gravity and mythic import to this well-worn fairy tale.

At the climax, when the Prince finally placed

the glass slipper on the Princess's foot and the ecstatic couple hugged and rode off to live happily ever after, the pig went wild with joy, danced around on his hind legs, and broke his silence by barking.

In rehearsal, the teacher had tried explaining to Norman that even if there was a pig in the Cinderella story, pigs don't bark. But as she expected, Norman explained that *this* pig barked.

And the barking, she had to admit, *was* well done.

The presentation at the teacher's conference was a smash hit.

At the curtain call, guess who received a standing ovation?

Of course. Norman, the barking pig.

Who was, after all, the *real* Cinderella story.

Word of a good thing gets around, and the kindergarten class had many invitations to come and perform Cinderella. Sometimes the teacher would have to explain what it was about the performance that was unique.

"It has a pig in it, you see?"

"Oh, really?"

"Yes, the star of the show is . . . a *barking* pig."

"But there's no barking pig in 'Cinderella.' "
"Well, there is now."

Here's a very different version of the Cinderella story. From a very different classroom. Its cast of characters are grown-ups; it's the school of hard knocks, and it happens on the street, not onstage.

"Mister, you got a sense of humor?"
"Sure."
"I'll tell you most of a joke for a nickel."
"Most of a joke?"
"Right. And then for twenty cents I'll tell you the punch line."
"What if I don't want to know the punch line?"
"Hey—it's up to you. Take a chance, give me a nickel—what have you got to lose?"

Whenever I walk across this small city park, I get hit for a handout by those we commonly label "winos"—those burned-out, torn edges of the fabric of urban life who use this green square as an office, bedroom, social club, and toilet. As one explained to me, "We've gone to the dogs and even the dogs don't want us." The usual request is a muttered "Spare

change?" or a more specific asking for a quarter for coffee. To cross the park is to cross an
invisible toll bridge. I pay. And sometimes get
a kind of fraternal blessing for my coin. "God
bless you, brother."

It is not a joyful matter, this awkward asking
and giving. And I know I could choose to walk
around, instead of through, the park. Yet they
are there, and I know it. I have spare change,
and they know it. So we do what is to be done
in the world-as-it-is-just-now. No matter what
one does on behalf of the down-and-out and
homeless, there is always this inescapable
one-human-being-to-another   engagement.
This asking hand outstretched. At those times
I cannot walk by and think or say that I gave
money to some fund and voted for some laws
and that I've done enough. I'd like to, but it just
doesn't work that way.

Back to the park and the man offering part of
a joke. I gave him a nickel, and he gave me a
tale about a rabbi, a nun, a pig, and a chicken
in a phone booth in Detroit. Outrageous joke.
And he told it so well that I paid him five bucks
for the punch line. It was a bargain. I laughed
most of the rest of the afternoon as the story
came back to mind. And I sent a few friends
around to the park to check it out. I wasn't

about to tell them the joke *or* the punch line for free.

The next day I learned that a small-scale vaudeville show was now part of the life of the park. A waitress in one of the nearby cafés, who daily went to smoke a cigarette there on her coffee breaks, befriended several of the winos. She actually talked to them.

She thought they were people. She convinced them to be more creative with their panhandling. They could be making twice as much for the same effort and have some fun as well. Why not? What did they have to lose?

This explains Mr. Part-of-a-Joke.

Other offerings from the cast include short poems, songs, advice, directions, excuses, card tricks, and quick fortunes. One guy offers to "laugh *with* you or *at* you for twenty-five cents." People now are attracted to the park who once avoided it. The new spirit may not last long, but for the time being, it is springtime there.

That waitress is a fairy godmother.

Not armed with a fancy magic wand, but with *compagination*—compassion mixed with imagination.

She touched the winos—not on their heads, but on their self-respect.

She did not give them pumpkins or shoes, but ideas about how they might come by these things.

She did not solve their problems but re-solved the problem of food for one day.

She urged them to fish instead of begging for fishbones.

She offered them a glimpse of the truth that there are always options—which is called hope.

I've never much liked the conventional Cinder-ella story. Not the one that's most commonly told in the United States. The American Cin-derella is a victim of bad luck. Her mother dies. Her father remarries badly—to a wicked woman with two narcissistic daughters. Cin-derella is relegated to the role of mistreated servant, sleeping on the ash heap by the hearth. There's nothing she can do but accept her fate.

About all Cinderella does is wish for luck, even though she doesn't expect any. She doesn't run away. She doesn't sabotage her living companions with clever moves. She doesn't cut their evil hearts out with a steak knife, which is what they deserve. Oh, no, nothing of the sort. Cinderella is a nice girl. She wimps around and takes it. She's *waiting* for something to happen *to* her.

For no particular reason, the fairy god-mother shows up so Cinderella can go danc-ing up at the king's house. Cinderella doesn't ask, "Where the hell have you been, lady, and how about some warm underwear and a cou-ple of cheeseburgers with a side of fries in-stead of some see-through slippers and a ride in a jazzed-up pumpkin?"

Oh, no, none of that. Cinderella does just what she's told and goes off to the dance.

Now I'd think twice about trying to dance in glass shoes, but I'm not Cinderella. And I'd think twice about dancing with some unknown cutie-pie who showed up at my party in glass shoes; at least the fairy godmother could have come up with *dancing* shoes—gold lamé alli-gator pumps with a strap across the instep. But then, I'm not the Prince, either, and appar-ently the fairy godmother had the Prince pretty well figured out. Because the Prince went out of his mind over Cinderella, and you know what happened next.

Cinderella sits home and waits. Never says a word about where she's been or what she knows. She waits.

"Maybe something will happen" is Cinder-ella's motto. She waits some more.

Until the Prince shows up. Him with the foot fetish. He doesn't look in the door and see two ugly girls and one dirty one and move on. Oh, no, not him. He doesn't care about beauty or character or cleanliness. It's the right foot he's looking for. And Cinderella doesn't care either. If it's what the Prince wants, then she's going to go along with it.

"And they lived happily ever after," says the story. I don't think so.

We always come in at the middle of a story and always have to leave before it really ends. In fairy stories. In the history of the world. The story always goes on. Shoe size is a lousy basis for love, but maybe Cinderella could live with that, and who knows? Stranger marriages than hers have made it, and maybe the Prince and Cinderella did die happy, with thousands of pairs of shoes.

But as a fairy tale for the young, I'll take any one of about five hundred other versions of this drama over the one we know best. Because most of the rest have an active heroine, who takes the initiative and works for her release from bondage. She doesn't just sit there. She knows she's got class and she understands that the relatives she's living with are dirtbags, and she isn't counting on anybody else to do something about her situation. In all

the European versions, Cinderella looks for a
way out by being clever and by being true to
the good memory of her noble mother. It's true
she has good luck, but it's also true that she
deserves it. She goes for the slipper in the
end—"Here, that's mine, let me try it on," she
says. She even forgives her two stepsisters
and finds a couple of dukes for them to marry.
About the luck of such people as this Cinderella, we say it couldn't happen to anyone who
deserved it more.

> *The passive, helpless, waiting version*
>   *of Cinderella is poison.*
> *Even God is more likely to help those*
>   *who help themselves.*
> *Norman, the barking pig, is my idea of*
>   *Cinderella.*
> *The teacher who recognized him is my*
>   *idea of royalty.*
> *And those who help winos help*
>   *themselves are my idea of fairy*
>   *godmothers.*
>
> *To insist on one's place in the scheme*
>   *of things and to live up to that place.*
> *To empower others in their reaching for*
>   *some place in the scheme of things.*
> *To do these things is to make fairy*
>   *tales come true.*

You might as well know now. A cigar is the centerpiece of what follows. And you might as well also know that I have been known to smoke one of those things from time to time, despite what I know about all the good reasons not to. I'm just assuming that you sometimes do something of your own that you shouldn't do, either, and will understand. Moreover, I only had one puff from this cigar. Yet it was the cigar I will never forget.

One fine fall morning in San Francisco. I had taken a cable car from Union Square to the foot of Columbus Street, intending to walk back through the old Italian quarter of North Beach. In a great mood. A week of hard work had gone well, and now I had a couple of days off to myself. So I had gone into Dunhill's and bought the finest cigar in the shop to smoke on an equally fine walk.

If you happen to appreciate cigars, this was a Macanudo, maduro, as big around as my thumb and six-and-a-half inches long—a very serious cigar. If you do not appreciate cigars, this one is best described as one of those cigars that would make you say, "My God, you're not going to smoke that thing in here, are you?"

After a few blocks' walk, it was cigar time. With care I removed the cellophane, squeezed the cigar to check for freshness, and held it to my nose to make sure it wasn't sour. Perfect. Leaning against a tree, I cut the end off the cigar with my pocketknife and carefully lit up. One puff, and I said aloud to myself: "Now that, THAT, is *some* cigar!"

It so happened that I had been standing in front of a coffeehouse. A cup of fine espresso would add the final right ingredient to a recipe for a memorable morning. Placing the lit cigar carefully on the wide brick window ledge of the coffeehouse, I went inside to order. While waiting at the counter, I glanced out the window to check on my cigar. Gone. My cigar was gone.

Abandoning my coffee, I rushed to the door. And stopped short. There on the other side of the glass was an old man examining my cigar with the skill of an aficionado. He held the cigar with respect under his nose and smelled it with eyes closed. He smiled. He squeezed the cigar to check for freshness. He smiled. Looking carefully up and down the street, he took a puff. And smiled again. With a heaven-ward salute with the cigar, he set off down the street. SMOKING MY CIGAR. I followed, not knowing quite what to do. I really wanted that cigar back.

The old man. Salt-and-pepper hair, with grand mustache and eyebrows to match—jaunty black longshoreman's cap, white long-sleeved shirt, black suspenders, and dark brown pants and shoes. Short, plump, wrin-kled, walking with a slight limp, the old man ambled on into the morning, unaware of me lurking furtively a few yards behind.

Italian. First-generation immigrant probably. As were the friends he visited to report the good news of the cigar that fate had prepared for him that fine day. I got a tour of the old Italian quarter of North Beach I had not antici-pated—the real thing. A pasta shop, a fruit stand, a hardware store, a bakery, and the local priest. At each stop, in passionate terms, he exalted the cigar, his good fortune, and this lovely day. Each friend was offered a sample puff. The fruit vendor squeezed the cigar and approved its ripeness. The baker puffed twice and pronounced the cigar *"Primo, primo."* The priest gave the cigar a mock blessing.

In time the old man turned toward the bocce ball courts north of Ghirardelli Square, and when he arrived, he repeated for his compatriots his ritual celebration of the cigar and his good luck. The cigar burned down to a short stub. As it came his turn to play, the old man meditated upon the end of the cigar with clear regret. He did not toss it to the ground and grind it underfoot as I might have. No. Solemnly, he walked over to a flower bed, scooped a small hole beneath a rosebush, laid the cigar butt to rest, covered it with dirt, and patted the small grave smooth with his hand. Pausing, he raised his cap in respect, smiled, and returned to play the game.

The old man may have smoked it, but I've not enjoyed a cigar more. If having a lovely memory is the best possession, then that cigar is still mine, is it not? It remains the very finest cigar I never had.

*H*iccup. Or hiccough, if you want to be stylish. *Hikke* is what the Danes write. In Spanish, *hipo*. *Hoquet* in French. *Shihuk* is Hebrew. And the Russians say *iknutz*. *Singhiozzo* in Italian. And *singultus* is the term doctors use—it's Latin, of course, nicely avoiding the whole problem of getting the sound right. But, like sneezes, yawns, burps, and farts, hiccups are usually benign, self-limiting events of more concern to amateur therapists than the serious medical community.

"A contraction of the abdominal and thoracic respiratory musculature, particularly the diaphragm." "A diaphragmatic spasm causing a sudden inhalation which is interrupted by the spasmodic closure of the glottis." That pretty well sums up the technical description of hiccups. I haven't found any good hiccup stories in joke books. No quotations in Bartlett's either. The medical literature is comparatively thin, as well—dealing mostly with chronic cases and desperate measures of cure, including surgery. Seems odd that such a common and socially powerful phenomenon is so overlooked in literature.

Hiccups have been recognized as a medical concern since Hippocrates' time, and though they are associated with an almost unlimited number of diseases, conditions, and circumstances, nobody knows what causes them. There are as many cures as there are apparent causes. Everybody hiccups. Even infants still in the womb hiccup. The reason most cures work at some time on some people is that hiccups usually last from between seven and sixty-three hics before stopping of their own accord. Whatever you do to pass the time while the episode runs its course seems to qualify as a "cure," so the more entertaining the cure is, the better. It's a self-limiting condition. Like the common cold, which will usually run its course in seven days if you do nothing and which will also clear up in about a week if you follow medical advice.

However. If you don't stop around sixty hics, then you have a chronic case and have moved into the major leagues of hiccup history. The *Guinness Book of World Records* reports the case of Charles Osborn of Anthon, Iowa, who has hiccuped every twelve minutes since 1922. It started when he was slaughtering a pig. He's led an ordinary life otherwise. Got married and had children and so on. Mostly the hiccups bother him now because he has trouble keeping his false teeth firmly in place when he hics. Despite the best efforts of the medical community, no cause or cure has been found for Mr. Osborn's hiccups. He has received tens of thousands of letters offering an astonishing range of cures. Other than the equally vexing common cold, no medical problem has as many prescriptions for treatment.

My own interest in hiccups lies in their social context. Hiccup Power. The capacity of hiccups for changing the dynamics in any gathering of people. I am fascinated by what happens in a room full of people when this phenomenon occurs. Hiccups are an instant attention-getting device. Just hiccup a couple of times and those around you will rush to your aid, offering cures and interventions. A case of hiccups will alter a cocktail party from a bus-stop mood of lethargic small talk to an emergency-room atmosphere. People will offer to pound on your back, bring you water, or put a paper bag over your head, among other things. "Stand on your head," "Hold your breath," "Jump up and down," and all the rest. People will start telling hiccup stories and sharing remedies. The hiccupper will be treated with great solicitation while in the throes of these miniconvulsions, and the shaman who has come up with the winning cure will be looked upon with the respect accorded witch doctors and faith healers. A new vitality will have come upon the group, energizing it. Above all, people will laugh. Hiccups are funny.

(NOTE: Since there is no adequate written expression for the real sound each individual makes when hiccuping, I would like to ask your help in bringing life to the following story. As you read to yourself, please make the appropriate hiccup *sound aloud in your own way whenever you encounter the word* hiccup *in the text. From experience, I can tell you it works out especially well if there is another person in the room with you while this is going on.)*

. . .

It happened at a wedding. Serious wedding. A by-the-book wedding that was beginning to get long and tedious. The time came for the vows, and the bride turned her pale face toward me.

"Please repeat after me: I, Mary, do take you, Jack, to be my husband."

And the bride responded.

"I *(hiccup),* Mary, do take you *(hiccup),* John, to be my *(hiccup).* . . ."

Somebody in the back of the church giggled. A couple of sniggers were heard. I looked at the congregation and saw row after row of tight-upper-lip grins. A few had their hands locked onto their mouths. Uh-oh.

I paused. Took a deep breath. Composed my face and mind. Waited for things to settle down. The congregation reached deep down inside for control. The bride repressed her spasms, subtly twitching from time to time as if receiving a slight electric shock near her navel. Her life energy had shifted from the awesome experience of getting married to the simple matter of controlling her diaphragm and glottis.

A little voice in the back of my head warned me that we were sitting on a social time bomb here, and if the bride opened her mouth and laid one more *hiccup* on us, we were going over the falls. Time stood still.

I weighed my options. I could acknowledge her condition, call for some water, and ask everyone else to take a deep breath. People would smile, chuckle politely, relax, and the wedding could go on by the book. Or, I could cover up the problem and simply say the vows myself and ask the bride and groom to say "yes" or just give me an affirmative nod. I like to think that I surely must have considered these options before I decided to go ahead and "let 'er buck" as we used to say in the rodeo.

Looking straight at the bride, deadpan, I continued: "In good times, and in bad."

The bride, bless her heart, went for it: "In good times *(hiccup)*, and in *(hiccup)* . . ."

Somebody in the front row tried to suppress a giggle and failed. Someone else let out one of those expelled-air sounds diesel locomotives make when they release their brakes. And a guy about ten rows back lost it. No giggler, he, but a belly laugher. To his credit, he tried for the exit before he blew, but he never made it. Waves of laughter sloshed back and forth across the church. I laughed, the bride and groom laughed, and the attendants likewise. Up in the choir loft the organist was hysterical. People rose out of their pews to breathe—people wept, snorted, brayed, hooted, howled, honked, and dabbed at their eyes with handkerchiefs. And every time some semblance of quiet and order seemed to be returning, the bride did it again. *"Hiccup,"* and pandemonium would resume.

Finally, fifteen minutes later, when the last ounce of laughter had been squeezed from us and the congregation looked more like survivors of a shipwreck than a wedding party, I held up my hand for silence and said that if weddings were supposed to be joyful human events, then we had exceeded all hopes and expectations for an acceptable level of joy. I said we all knew what the words were and what they meant, and in the spirit of those words I pronounced the couple man and wife and blessed their marriage.

In response, the bride blurted out, "Oh *(hiccup)*, thank you." And the guy in the back lost it again, and the bride and groom raced down the aisle with the laughter that was their recessional music, since the organist was no longer functional.

Thank God for these real-life accidents that keep us from the boredom of perfection. I will never forget when a similar thing happened at an inappropriately grim funeral once. An old uncle of the deceased got the *hiccups,* and when he tried to repress them, he managed to both *hiccup* and *fart* at the same time. You can't really ignore these things, try as you might, even under funeral conditions. Uncle Jack saved the day. Great funeral.

(I hope, in carrying out your responsibilities to make the appropriate sounds as they appear in the text, that your capacities haven't been overtaxed here.)

*T*here is a tree. At the downhill edge of a long, narrow field in the western foothills of the La Sal Mountains—southeastern Utah. A particular tree. A juniper. Large for its species— maybe twenty feet tall and two feet in diameter. For perhaps three hundred years this tree has stood its ground. Flourishing in good seasons, and holding on in bad times. "Beautiful" is not a word that comes to mind when one first sees it. No naturalist would photograph it as exemplary of its kind. Twisted by wind, split and charred by lightning, scarred by brush- fires, chewed on by insects, and pecked by birds. Human beings have stripped long strings of bark from its trunk, stapled barbed wire to it in using it as a corner post for a fence line, and nailed signs on it on three sides: NO HUNTING; NO TRESPASSING; PLEASE CLOSE THE GATE. In commandeering this tree as a corner stake for claims of rights and property, miners and ranchers have hacked signs and symbols in its bark, and left Day-Glo orange survey tape tied to its branches. Now it serves as one side of a gate between an alfalfa field and open range. No matter what, in drought, flood, heat, and cold it has continued. There is rot and death in it near the ground. But at the greening tips of its upper branches and in its berrylike seed cones, there is yet the outreach of life.

I respect this old juniper tree. For its age, yes. And for its steadfastness in taking whatever is thrown at it. That it has been useful in a practical way beyond itself counts for much, as well. Most of all, I admire its capacity for self-healing beyond all accidents and assaults. There is a *will* in it—toward continuing to be, come what may.

Last night, I went out for a walk in the darkness of early autumn to check and see if someone had remembered to turn the Milky Way on and the wind off. Drawn back to the cabin by the yellow glow of a reading lamp in the living room, I stood outside the window for a long time and looked in at my wife curled up on the couch sewing a hem in a new pair of wool trousers for me.

For seventeen years she has been my companion, my friend, my co-conspirator.

Yesterday, we were outraged at one another over something that seems trivial now, but the fire of anger is not quite cooled beneath the surface ashes. Yesterday, I made her cry in frustration. Yesterday, she was mad at me. I know I drive her crazy sometimes. She's not always easy to live with either. Yesterday, old grievances were flung off the shelf where they are somewhat shakily stored.

Yet today we walked up the road to pick sweet corn from a neighbor's patch and walked back down the road hand in hand in our usual way. We're good at forgiving. We have to be. The weather of love comes and goes, and we must let it. It is a required condition of loving someone and being loved back.

And now, tonight, as I watch her through the window, I see her smile as she carefully fixes my trousers, perhaps thinking to make one leg slightly longer than the other in revenge.

The gate we passed through to pick corn was the one attached to the old juniper. And that tree comes to mind this night as I look in

on her. I long for the love we have to always
be like that tree. With a steadfast ability to take
it—a capacity for self-healing and growing on,
scars and all, come what may.

"How was your walk, dear?" she asks as I
come through the door.

"The stars are still there.

"The wind is calmed.

"And there's still enough light to see trees."

"Tell me a love story out of your life—from
high school or college days."

"Are you serious?"

"Yes. I'm interested in very short love
stories—I want to write some."

And the person questioned will smile and
get a faraway look in her eyes as her true
confession unravels.

The plots of these dramas are familiar. But
details are wonderfully unique.

The love that was never meant to be—unre-
quited love—is the most common theme.

In high school one learns that love is not
forever. One may even go to college with a
new attitude and look for love, fully counting
on its being temporary, intending to taste the
fruit of many trees. Yet love has a way of am-
bushing the heart and folding the best-laid

plans back in upon the planner. None of these love affairs ends in a tidy way. Never did you come to the end of the school term, politely thank each other for the course in love, and sign up for something else. Everybody gets burned sometime. Everybody gets a turn.

For example:

In her freshman year she volunteered for the committee to introduce computer dating to campus. Her real motive was to have first chance at the material and then tweak the computer to make her out to be the perfect match for the hottest hunk on campus. She picked out the man of her dreams. Mr. Wonderful. A senior. Everything he said about himself fit her profile. She had always been in love with this man.

She cooked the books, and the computer arranged a date two weeks away. For fourteen beautiful days and fourteen beautiful nights she was in love as she had never been in love before.

One flaw in all this. Men lie. Yes. Especially those desperate enough to turn to computer dating in their senior year in college.

One look and it was "uh-oh." Yes, he was a toad. Of course he was. Not even kissing him would have helped. He admitted he was desperate. He admitted that he lied. Also, in preparation for this moment of truth, he had tossed down several straight shots of vodka, so even the sincerity of his confession was suspect. Twenty years later, at their college reunion, he apologized again. That's when she finally admitted fiddling with the books in the first place.

She's not sorry about the two weeks before he showed up, though. In a way he was re-sponsible for one of the best two weeks of her life—the imagined possibility of a totally con-suming love with a magnificent man. Nothing real ever quite lived up to that. It didn't last long, but it was the best love affair she ever had.

> *Falling in love with love is falling for*
> *   make-believe.*
> *Falling in love with love is playing the*
> *   fool.*

Right. Count us all in. At least once. How else could we know it's true?

Ely, Nevada. East side of the great open emp-tiness of high desert basin and range country. Intersection of U.S. highways 6, 93, and 50. The latter is called "the loneliest highway in America," and I believe it. I drove 140 miles

(Oh my.)

"What's someone as pretty as you doing in a place like this?" I asked.

(I can't believe I said that—it's like I'm in *Gunsmoke* talking to Miss Kitty.)

"I'm in sales."

(Was Miss Kitty in sales? Is this a movie? Am I on camera?)

"What kind of sales?"

"What would you like to buy?"

I laughed. She laughed.

"Actually, I shouldn't have said that—I'm not really open for business right now. Not until after three o'clock."

"That's funny hours—how late do you work?"

"Until three or four o'clock in the morning."

"Those are long hours—do you sell door to door?"

I laughed. She laughed. The cook is laughing as he comes out of the kitchen with the orders of huevos rancheros. Hers in a plastic box and mine in a plate the size of a broiling pan.

"You haven't spent much time around here, have you?"

"Why?"

"Well, it's either that or else you're a whole lot dumber than you look. I'm a professional prostitute. Anybody can see that. I work at a chicken ranch seven miles east of Ely. Like I say, I'm not open for business until three, and maybe not even after that if you really are as dumb as you look."

And out the door she went.

The cook said, "You're in for a hard day, bubba, if you don't watch out. Take a tip from a guy who knows—that lady is certain heartbreak and these huevos rancheros is certain heartburn. I'd just move on down the road, if I was you."

Not wanting any kind of heart trouble, I took the cook's advice.

So much for love at first sight. I don't mind knowing what she did for a living. But it hurt knowing I am as dumb as I look.

Then, there was this lady truck driver. Another Ohmy. Cute. Small space between her front teeth when she smiled. What color eyes? I don't know. She wore sunglasses all the time. Every day she had on a sleeveless green blouse and I could see her muscles working as she turned the wheel of her truck. How tall was she? Don't know. She was sitting up there inside the cab of the truck every time I saw her. And hers was a big truck. I mean BIG truck. One of those huge double-dump rigs used in major excavations.

What else do I know? She drank orange juice straight—out of a half-gallon plastic jug she kept in the cab beside her, and read books sitting in the cab while the guy driving the Caterpillar loader filled her dumpers with dirt. And I know that she could really wheel and deal with her truck—charge into that construction site, jack her rig around into just the right place the first try, and then roar off again, moving through ten gears so easy I couldn't tell when she shifted.

I know all this because three days in a row on the way to work I got stopped by a flagman while the lady truck driver came and went. I guess I saw her all of about three minutes in three days.

But I fell in love with her. She set off my bells and whistles. I like attractive, independent, competent women, and I like truck drivers. And she was both.

I imagined meeting her in some little truck-stop café and her saying to me:

"Hey, aren't you that handsome man I saw in the dark blue '52 panel truck on Eastlake three days in a row? I can't believe I'm lucky enough to meet you here."

Never happened. Never will. It's just as well. I wouldn't know what to do next.

The excavation is finished, and she's moving dirt somewhere else now, I guess.

But I miss her. And our three-day, three-minute love affair.

It wasn't meant to be, but while it was, it was memorable.

If we were talking together in the same room, it would be time now for your own short love stories. If you've got a good one, write it down and send it to me.

You don't have to remind me. I'm fifty-three years old, very happily married, a grandfather, and a semirespectable citizen not really looking for more trouble than I can handle. But short love stories are a special interest of mine. Especially if the event takes place in my imagination. I don't mind being a controlled romantic.

This is not an easy subject to discuss. It's open to misinterpretation in a major way. I recall Jimmy Carter getting into all kinds of trouble because he was candid enough to tell a *Playboy* magazine interviewer that, yes, he did occasionally look upon another woman with desire in his heart. It was a normal human thing to do, he thought. He said he never acted upon such feelings or intended to. The journalists made a lot of hay out of that statement, as if we wouldn't want somebody like that as president. But I and a whole lot of other people hurry and the yarn gets all tangled. We cannot see to untangle it, so we keep going, hoping it will reach the rest of the way. By being careful, going slowly, stretching the yarn around corners and over a wall, working together, we just manage to tie the ends together. The circle of white string is complete. We shout in triumph. We did it!

As I say, I don't know what all this means.

I do know this. It's another love story. The next morning, I went up the hill to the house just after daybreak. The coals in the fire were still hot. The string still held. And on the backside of the house, where the darkness was, the string had knots and tangles and was stretched almost to breaking. We could not have fixed it last night—the tangles in darkness had to remain part of the string or we could have never gone on all the way around. God bless the master of this house, the mistress bless also . . . tangles and all.

*F*or several children in our neighborhood, this is that very special summer between their seventh and eighth year—between first and second grade. They have been to school. And they have been out in the world for a while on their own five days a week—walking home from school.

The age of exploration has come. And they have explored every inch of their environment at home when their parents weren't looking: scouting out the attic, garage, closets, bureau drawers, purses and wallets, and the glove compartments of cars. They have played what-would-happen-if? with electric appliances, and can tell you what becomes of Play-

Doh in the toaster, how far away from the house the stereo can be heard if it is turned full volume, and what the microwave does to Jell-O if you leave it in long enough. Throw in some baseball cards, the daily walk to the corner store, a little minor theft, and it's summertime.

A fine summer. Daring—pushing the edge. Daily, they wander off a little further into the neighborhood than their parents allow—crossing streets they should not cross, throwing rocks at dogs and cats, going through alleys instead of along front sidewalks. Up on roofs and up in trees, down in basements, into neighbors' houses, and out in rowboats. It is the summer of mischief and the crossing of forbidden frontiers. Far more independent and adventuresome and curious and courageous than their parents realize or want to remember.

Last week I saw three of these kids hiding in the bushes up by the road with their bathing suits on. Shouting, they would leap out of the bushes, drop their shorts to moon passing cars, and then run into the nearest backyard to fall on the ground, shrieking and laughing at their bravado and their defiance of taboos. Nothing more daring—nothing more hilarious—than to wave their small white butts at the passing traffic and run for cover.

To them, I am only "Old Fulghum"—harmless enough, even though *they* know *I* know what they're up to because I'm around during the day and come and go unpredictably, unlike their parents, most of whom are at work. I mind my business, and they mind theirs. We have an unspoken nonintervention pact.

This week they are playing with fire.

In a vacant lot, with boxes of wooden matches and a roll of toilet paper. Burning one sheet at a time and watching the flaming ash rise in the air and float away. Entranced. Fascinated. Playing with fire—taunting danger. As I watch them, I hear no laughing—this is a serious event.

When I was teaching art in a high school, I held a high card in my teacher's deck that I always saved to deal in the doldrums of late spring when learning had dropped to a minimal level and the daily classroom experience was mostly an exercise in crowd control. My ace in the hole. Fire.

We had Fire Day.

Each student was issued a full box of wooden matches and an electric glue gun, and was required to use every match to build a structure of some sort—something creative.

The assignment was to see how large a construction could be built from one box of matches. Prizes for the highest, longest, most aesthetically pleasing, plus a booby prize for the stupidest contraption. There was always a lot of competition for the booby prize.

The following day we would carry the creations out behind the gymnasium, and there on the rubbly, dry ground in back of the gym, the sculptural masterpieces would be set afire, one at a time. We watched, hypnotized, as matter turned to energy—as what was *something* became *nothing.* As what had started out as imagination and became substance was changed into memory.

On one occasion we accidentally set fire to the dry grass and leaves around us. Somebody in the school office saw the smoke and both called the fire department and set off the school fire alarms. The whole school turned out to see what was burning. It was hard explaining the educational aspects of the project to the firemen. For the students, having a fire drill as the climax of Fire Day was a maximum event.

When asked to evaluate the course, Fire Day was high on the students' list of successful educational projects. This primitive and ritualistic handling of a taboo buried so deep in their genetic wiring was difficult to express in words. The inelegance of their writing was balanced by the fiery intensity of feelings expressed in their papers.

I explained that they were—and the whole of existence was—fire-born.

Life is—and we are—byproducts of combustion.

Imagination turned to form and finally, memory.

This whole world once was fire. A flaming ball of molten rock. Lava. The whole thing. The ultimate ecological disaster. And still it is on fire—at the center of the earth, far beneath our feet, the fire rages on.

The big bang that birthed us—that was fire.

And we are told, by scientist and religious prophet alike, that the Big Bang that ends us is also fire. Next time.

Fire may be a no-no to seven-year-olds, but it is Yes-Yes to life itself.

I spent an evening focused on fireflies recently. Sitting in a wicker chair on the high bank about a hundred feet above the Pai River in the north of Thailand, near the Burma border. Early evening, sometime in January 1990, and maybe on a Sunday. My vagueness is due to being a long way from urban Western civilization for several weeks, and having lost track of time. Which is what I came to do.

No television, no radio, no newspapers, no telephones, no fax machines. UPS doesn't even deliver there. Not much to do at night but sit still and smoke cheap Thai cigars (sixty for about ten cents) and sip some Singha beer and watch fireflies. Not very exciting. Which is great if the last thing you want in the world at the moment is excitement.

The tree in front of me was full of fireflies— as though somebody had overdone it and put too many little tiny white lights on a Christmas tree. And, I kid you not, the fireflies were doing synchronized flashing. All together. On. Off. On. Off. My Thai host said they were all males "calling out for love."

One of these little flashers landed on my pillow when I went to bed. So I put a water glass over him and watched him up close. And wondered:

Just how much control does a firefly have
    over his stern light?
Could one be trained to do Morse code
    and be worked into a flea-circus act?

Does a firefly ever attract teeny-tiny
    moths?
Is his light like the stars and always there,
    only we can't see it in the daylight?
Does the firefly enjoy getting turned on, or
    is it more like having hiccups—just an
    urgent, involuntary spasm?
Do fireflies come with different wattage,
    like light bulbs?
Do firefly bulbs burn out, leaving old fire-
    flies to wander around in the dark, un-
    noticed and unloved?
What might it be like if we humans were
    similarly equipped? What kind of pants
    would we have to wear?

I know some people who give off a lot of
light. Because they have absorbed a lot of light
themselves. They shine. This is not the kind of
light you can actually see with your eyes, of
course. But there are lots of parts of the spec-
trum of light we can't see. We experience the
results of its existence. It takes a different kind
of looking.

To look this way is to see.
To see is to have vision.
To have vision is to understand.
To understand is to know.

To know is to become.
To become is to live fully.
To live fully is to matter.
And to matter is to become light.
And to become light is to be loved.
And to be loved is to burn.
And to burn is to exist.
Off and on.

Maybe the fireflies are on to something.

*I*n the dusty yellow light of an early summer morning, in the shade of graceful old trees in the forecourt of an ill-kept temple, three small girls are offering little clay amulets tied to small bamboo cages containing tiny birds to those who come to pray. This is northwest Thailand. The valley of the Pai River. The town of Mae Hong Son. Ten kilometers from the Burma border. I see the bird-sellers each morning as I walk from my lodgings nearby to have break-fast in the only café in town where English is somewhat spoken.

The birds are not actually for sale in the sense that you can take them home with you. When you give the little girls a few baht, you are entitled to set one of the birds free and thereby add to your achievement of merit. You keep the amulet as evidence of your act—a kind of ecclesiastical receipt for a righteous act.

A cynical mind might conclude that here is one more example of the scams worked by organized religion on the young and/or gullible. The selling of indulgences is ubiquitous and continuous the world over. Even Martin Luther's whistle-blowing didn't change the matter much in the Western world. Here in Buddhist Thailand the tradition continues.

I express that opinion to my breakfast host.

In a verbal puzzle of Thai, English, and German he explains that not only have I missed the whole point of the bird enterprise, but I don't know all I need to know about how the operation really works. Please to come with him to the temple.

"Now? Before I finish my toast?"

"Now. This is important. You will digest your breakfast better if you know."

We returned to the temple—not to the salesgirls out front, but around back. On an old wooden table is the rest of the story. A pan of water, and several uninhabited bamboo cages with bread crumbs just inside the open doors.

When the sparrows are freed out front, they fly around the temple to the table, take a drink of water, hop into a cage to eat the crumbs, and another little girl gently closes the cage and places it in a larger basket to be carried back around front.

My breakfast guru explains that this is not an official business of the temple—but it is in harmony with the purposes of the temple, so it is allowed. The little girls provide food and water for the birds, the birds provide an opportunity for a religious gesture to those who come to pray, and they, in turn, provide a small income for the little girls. It is no secret how the matter works, and no hypocrisy is involved—everyone has a part in an enterprise to which everyone gives and from which everyone is given. I see that the bird business is nonviolent, ecologically sound, and existentially meaningful as a metaphor for the great circle of being.

"Do you get it?" my teacher asks.

"I get it," say I, wondering how I missed it in the first place.

Then he asks if knowledge of the full cycle of the bird business has affected my cynicism. That's the heart of religious questing, isn't it? Once you get a handle on the infinite cycle of the restless existence of all things, do you despair or do you willingly take your place in the circle? Does enlightenment lead to sorrowful disengagement or willing participation? Once you know where the roller coaster is going, are you still in for the ride?

As my friend has promised, what he had to show me was indeed important and did affect my breakfast. The eating became a meditation. I ate everything but the toast, which was dry and crumbly by now. Took the toast with me to the temple. Around to the back. Gave it to the little girl. "This is for the birds," I said, taking my place in the wholesale end of the merit market.

   Give and it shall be given unto you, since the gifts go around and back again.

*L*ourdes, Mecca, Jerusalem, Benares, Ise, Canterbury, Salt Lake City. All famous destinations of religious pilgrimage. Holy places, temples, shrines, cathedrals—containing relics, books, and wisdom. Saints, sutras, the smell of incense, high priests, stained-glass windows, great processions, and great revelations come to mind.

My own sacred city may be Pocatello, Idaho. There's an invisible shrine there in the middle of an aisle of an Albertson's grocery store. Where the canned meats are—right in front of the tuna fish, to be specific. Once in a while I go there in my mind—and I wish someday to make a pilgrimage to go stand at that place once more and see if what happened last time might happen again.

In the summer of 1978, my wife was in her third year of medical school. She drew a clerkship assignment for six weeks of in-service training in pediatrics at a clinic in Pocatello. Located in the Portneuf Valley just off the great Snake River plains, this town is the Bannock County seat, and the home of Idaho State University. Once a stopping place on the Oregon Trail, then a major junction yard for the Union Pacific Railroad, the town also has a place in the history of vaudeville.

Since I like Idaho, the history of the Oregon Trail, railroads, vaudeville, universities, and my wife, I thought I'd go along to Pocatello. Besides, I had just crossed the frontier of the great plains of those over forty years of age and was looking for a route across. I wasn't quite sure where I was or where I was going, but wasn't too worried about it, either. My journey had a kind of pleasant aimlessness that may have been either a sign of wisdom or weariness, I wasn't sure which. Pocatello, Idaho, seemed like as good a place as any to be in my condition. Pocatello? Sure. Why not.

So. I went.

Since it was August, the university was not

in session, but its library was open. The library was air-conditioned. And since the August heat was well over 100 degrees in the afternoons, I spent six hours a day in the library. Usually, I had the whole library to myself. Except for a skeleton crew of librarians, who were eager to have one customer, the library was mine.

I decided my project would be at least to touch or pick up and consider every single book in the library. One Monday morning about ten-thirty, I began at the top floor at the far end of the first row in the stacks and headed out into the great forest of All Human Knowledge.

Despite my ambitious intentions, I didn't get far before accumulating an armload of books I wanted to look into further, and by noon each day I was settled in behind mounds of books at a big table on the third floor. The legendary scholar Fuljumowski, at work. Imagine—no papers to write, no exams . . . just learning. No college course I ever took gave me as much knowledge or as much pleasure as those days in that library. Anything I wanted to know was mine. As I walked home in the evening, a traveler on my own Oregon Trail, filled with experiences of that great country of the mind, I had an overwhelming bad news/good news feeling: Knowledge and the number of books that contained it were infinite—I could *never* read them *all.* And as I read one, ten more were being written somewhere. That was the bad news. The good news was that knowledge and the books that contained it were indeed infinite. I would *never* run out of things to learn. Knowledge was infinite in every direction I turned. The ultimate comfort for an autodidact.

One Friday evening, in this reflective mood, I stopped off at the Albertson's grocery store on my way home. Watermelon on my mind. Big watermelon. Take it home and eat the whole thing out in the yard. There was something else I was supposed to get, but could not recall, so I started walking up and down the aisles of the grocery store in much the same spirit as I had stalked the library shelves. And the same thing happened. Bad news and good news about groceries.

All this food—more than I could ever eat or taste—involving thousands of people from all over the world to get it here on the shelves—infinite in every direction because thousands of other people would come and get it and take it home and eat it at thousands of dinners and it would fuel their lives to do millions of things and I could only have just the barest comprehension of this immense complexity.

I picked up the first object in front of me—a can of tuna fish—and thought about its contents, the can itself, and the label, and all the incredible learning and working and the machinery and the processes and the fishing boats and fishermen and factory ships and trains and trucks that brought it here from so far away.

Then there's the line of thought away from here in the direction yet to come—where would it all go?—where would it end up?—the can, the label, the fish, and the person who ate the fish, and on and on and on?

This is not how I usually spend my time in a grocery store. For a moment the rational monitor in my mind was warning: Uh-oh, you are losing your marbles.

Walking up the aisle, my eye was caught by the bold black-and-white headlines of an advertising placard, which said: WELL, YOU'RE NOT THE ONLY ONE!—and in smaller print it had something to say about the quest for a decent canned spaghetti sauce.

The headline fit my existential state. Yes, I thought to myself, I'm not the only one. Not the only one who ever got a flash of the big picture. Not the only one who understands how utterly amazing it all is. There is lots of testimony in those books up there in the library.

This is exactly what all those books are about.

Holding on to my sanity and the watermelon and the can of tuna fish with equal care, I stopped at the checkout counter and paid with a twenty-dollar bill. I noticed a handwritten note on the little cup where coins appear at the end of a transaction. The note said: "Please accept your change—take it with you." Here was yet another unexpected message. Yes, I thought to myself, I accept my change—and the changes yet to come. And I will take my change with me, wherever I go.

Turning to leave, I was confronted with still another sign. The automatic doors were broken. The sign said: PLEASE NOTE—THE ONLY WAY OUT IS IN.

As always, it is how one perceives the door that determines the coming and going. There are two journeys one must make to have balance—OUT there and IN here. One depends upon the other. Every exit is an entrance. The door swings both ways. The only way out is always in. To move on in the world as it is, one must turn to resources within.

Well, now. In the long, long ago, such a life experience would be described as having a vision. A common event back then. Those old guys in the Bible would have no trouble with my telling them about this. And we accept such moments as happening to those old guys. Even as late as Proust, with his madeleine. But to me? Now? This is the twentieth century. We make fun of such moments— "What have you been smoking?"

I sense—I know—that these moments of deep connection with the way things are— these brief flashes of understanding—are not only contemporary, but common. It's just hard to talk about them—like our night dreams and daydreams.

When asked in earnest, most people will tell a similar story. We have not changed that much in the last two thousand years. These private moments of knowing ultimately matter most. Wherever they happen, that place becomes holy ground.

I am not crazy. Or stoned. Or strange.

Tested with my own cynical skepticism and most rational mind, I know that experience one summer's eve in a grocery store in Pocatello was a permanent landmark in my journey onward. A time when I stood at the summit of a pass in my own mountains and could see far behind me and far ahead. The world stood out before me and in me—infinite in every direction.

Don't worry if this has happened to you. Worry if it doesn't.

*L*ast Friday morning I started a fire in my wood stove using the comics section out of the Sunday newspaper. In the shower I drew all over myself with some Silly Soap left behind by my granddaughter. For breakfast, I ate a bowl of Cheerios topped with jelly beans. And drank a glass of Goofy Grape—a fizzy drink for kids. For background sound, on the stereo, a tape of one of Woody Allen's comic monologues. A live performance, with a roomful of people yukking their heads off. Tossing my briefcase in the closet, I headed for the door without any baggage. Meant to walk to my office downtown. At a snail's pace. As I went out the door, I noticed my granddaughter's red-and-white beanie with a propeller on top. It didn't fit, but it didn't fall off, either. It looked like one of the coolest yarmulkes you've ever seen. I put it on my head to see if I could walk fast enough to make the propeller work. I could.

I'd had a bad week. A draining downward spiral of unfinished business matched by the rising smoke of grumpiness, which set off my uh-oh alarm. And after going to bed on Thursday night in a junkyard-dog state of mind, it seemed wise to make tomorrow a better day. Experience tells me that I can choose to do that. That I had better do it or I'll be sorry.

Under these same conditions in times past I would take a day off—make up an excuse—but I can't call in sick anymore. Because now I'm self-employed—I work for me, and I'd know I was lying. For the same reason, telling the boss to stuff it is masochistic. If my work is my life, then I can't quit my job or fire me because wherever I go, there I am again—the employee who won't ever go away.

No radical moves make sense—just some course adjustments are required. Beginning with breakfast and going to work. Anything I can do to lighten up. The winning move was the walk in the hat. It's very hard to stay depressed when you are walking along wearing a too-small beanie with a propeller on top. Not a lot of people have seen a middle-aged man dressed in suit and tie, wearing a beanie like mine. People in cars honked, waved, shouted, "Go gettum, Grandpa." And once, at a stop sign, four teenagers sang a full chorus of the Mickey Mouse Song to me and roared off laughing.

I figure the loss of my dignity, which was good for me, was balanced by the gain in amusement I gave other people. They got to work in a good humor. They had something to talk about over coffee. I came to think of my wearing the hat and walking to work as a public service.

As for my breakfast, I turn to Cheerios for the lightness of heart the name implies. As long as I can remember, I have eaten Cheerios, and my kids have eaten Cheerios. And now my grandchildren eat Cheerios. Even if Cheerios were bad for me, I would probably keep eating the cereal just for the name, but when a leading consumers' organization recently affirmed it as being nutritionally sound, I felt both uplifted and wise in my choice of breakfast cereals.

There is a phrase in my mind that I think I found on a Cheerios box many years ago when I spent more time reading cereal boxes than I do now. The phrase: "The minimum daily adult requirement." The makers of Cheerios were referring to the stuff in the cereal—protein, vitamins, and minerals.

But the phrase hit me one morning as having larger implications.

What *is* "the minimum daily adult requirement"?

What do I really have to have, day by day, to get by?

Pretty basic stuff comes up when you try to answer that.

I always think about that phrase when I'm putting my gear together for a long backpacking trip. If I'm going to carry everything I need on my back for a couple of weeks in the mountains, then great care must be taken in choosing what is essential and what is not. About fifty pounds of provisions and gear are all I can comfortably carry. The packing itself becomes focused on economy, efficiency, and well-being. I think in elemental terms. Water. Fire. Shelter. Food. Protection from wind, rain, heat, cold. First aid. Knife. And tools to find my way—compass and map. The quality of the trip depends a great deal upon what I can live without. Mr. Thoreau would agree.

. . .

That old question off the cereal box came up again this morning.

When I looked at the list of all the things I had to do today, I realized that few of them fell into the minimum daily adult requirement category. I was lost in the underbrush of busyness again. So I called in well. Parked my briefcase full of paperwork on the sidelines of my life, and walked to work unburdened, in no hurry, singing. Wearing my hat.

Nothing miraculous occurred—no epiphanies, no great encounters, and no visions. Just sidewalks and trees and scruffy grass and people and cloudy sky and hazy sun and dogs and smells of coffee brewing and autos exhausting. A few dandelions in cracks in the sidewalk. Nothing special.

About the jelly beans. On the Cheerios. I know this is probably not recommended by nutritionists. But I had never tried it before. And you never know. Somebody has to do the field-testing. The jelly beans were better than raisins, actually. If you want to check it out, I suggest the Jelly Belly brand, which comes in forty official flavors. My choice was a combination of apricot, banana, watermelon, and root beer. If you want a little zing in the mix, throw in a few jalapeño-flavored ones. A little Wow!

in the Cheerios. A little whoopee in the minimum daily requirement.

As long as we're on the subject of jelly beans. About a week later, my three-year-old grandchild and I were sorting a pound of mixed-flavors jelly beans on the kitchen table while listening to country-western music. It's an imprinting and bonding ritual. Long after this, I hope when she eats jelly beans and listens to country-western music, she will think fondly of her grandfather and happy times. But I don't know what she thinks at the moment. Except that she does not like jalapeño-flavored Jelly Bellys, which I do, and does like the toasted-marshmallow–flavored ones, which I do not. So we sort and trade. We have carefully tested all forty flavors of Jelly Bellys and discussed the merits of each. Likewise, we have listened to a lot of country-western music. So far, her notion of good country-western music is "Old MacDonald Had a Farm" sung by Captain Kangaroo. My work is cut out for me. It may be a long time before she identifies with Hank Williams and "Your Cheating Heart." That takes time. And experience.

I love this child. Red-haired and patient and gentle like her mother; fey and funny like her father. When she giggles, I hear him when he and I were young. I am part of this child. It may be only because we share genes and that we therefore smell familiar to each other—as simple as that: only pheromones—that we are tied together. It also may be that a part of me lives in her in some important way and someday, someday—well, anything's possible. But for now it's jelly beans and "Old MacDonald" that unite us.

There are little clues that my life is entering a new stage. My children are beginning to look middle-aged, and they pat me in a patronizing way for no apparent reason. I don't want to ask why they are patting me—I'll take all the affection I can get from them in any form they want to dish it up. But I'm not used to being patted yet.

The other clue of change is a sudden desire to take small children on excursions.

Enter the previously mentioned Sarah and an adventure that sounds like the title of a B-grade children's storybook. Grandfather and grandchild go to the zoo. First time. And we saw the lions and tigers and elephants and kangaroos and bears and gorillas and all the rest—every last living creature the zoo had to offer plus a few possibly dead ones.

She rode in the stroller and I pushed. The

next time we do this, I'm going to ride and she's going to push.

For all of my "Oh, Sarah, look at the whatevers," Sarah was most impressed with the pigeons that hung around the food stand. What she liked about pigeons was that she could almost touch them but not quite. No matter how carefully, cautiously, quietly, she approached, the pigeons always managed to move just one small step further out of reach. The space between her and the pigeons moved in concert with her. She could come so near and yet never completely close the distance. She spent most of the time at the zoo trying to bridge this moving space between her and the pigeons. All the rest of the animals were over there in another world—behind bars or moats or glass—not unlike the pictures in a book. But the pigeons were over here in her world, and would be made even more real if she could just get her hands on one.

"What would you do with one if you caught it, Sarah?"

She didn't know. Possessing was not in the plan, actually. Reaching for the pigeons was all that was important to her. Not catching, but pursuing, mattered.

Riding home in a thunderstorm, Sarah fell asleep in her car seat beside me. In her par-

ents' driveway, I sat in the car and looked for a long time at her face. Who is this child? I wondered. I want to know her. Now that I am older and wiser and have the time and patience I did not have as a father, I will approach her as she approaches the pigeons—carefully, cautiously, quietly, with perseverance. And wonder, as she does, how one can be so close and so forever far at the same time. She is not "mine" and never will be. Two people think of her as "their" daughter. At least four other people think of her as "their" granddaughter. But Sarah only belongs to herself. There will always be a moving space between us—an untraversable distance to be treated with respect. Sarah doesn't know what she would do if she actually caught a pigeon. I don't know what I'd do if I ever caught Sarah. To love something and to possess it are not the same thing.

Talking to her father the next day, I inquired of Sarah's report on our excursion.

"She's been talking a lot about pigeons, jelly beans, Old MacDonald, and chicken hearts. Are you sure you guys went to the zoo?"

"Yes. And that's nothing. Wait till we get back from the Aquarium. I bet there are some really amazing pigeons there."

A couple of mornings ago, the lady who lives in the houseboat across the way from me was really getting down with Aretha Franklin as the stereo pounded out "R-E-S-P-E-C-T." While washing dishes, the lady was singing along and doing a few good dance moves around her kitchen as Aretha shouted out her gospel-style rock and roll. The lady does not know I was watching her. Nor does she know I have often watched her as she bops around her kitchen singing and dancing. Though I'd like to tell her how much I appreciate her spirit-lifting performance, I'm afraid if I say anything, it will make her too self-conscious and I will have spoiled a good time for both of us.

Besides, she can't really sing. That's what she says. When we were organizing a neighborhood Christmas choir a couple of years ago, I invited her to join us, and she said she had a terrible voice and couldn't carry a tune in a bucket. "I can't sing—never could." How can this be? I have watched and heard her sing. I know better. In fact, most people I know claim they can't sing. Why is this? What's going on here?

Imagine how it would seem if our educational system evaluated students around sixth grade and if you did not have clear potential for playing tennis at a Wimbledon championship level, the school and the parents would say you are not now and never will be a tennis player, and that would be the end of tennis for you. No way! We think of sports as a lifetime activity essential to good health. We think that it's important that people play tennis or golf or basketball or hockey or at least run or walk at whatever level they can—for their own good— as long as they can. We don't eliminate organized sports around sixth grade for all except those who seem to have talent and great potential for excelling to the point where they can make a professional career of the activity. That would really be absurd.

Yet when it comes to singing, that's exactly what we do. From sixth grade through high school, and the rest of your life, if you haven't been labeled as having "talent" or a "good voice" or if you aren't stubborn about it, you will not sing in the choir. And you will grow up at best being a secret singer, as embarrassed to be caught doing it in public as picking your nose.

If you want to clear a roomful of guests at a party, simply announce that "we are all going to gather around the piano and sing songs." Good night. People will make self-deprecating statements about their vocal inadequacies and head for the kitchen, bathroom, or just go on home.

Same is true on a camping trip. "Let's all sit around the campfire and sing" sends most people into their tents in a hurry. Unless they are old people. Who were around before radio or TV or stereos. And don't know any better. But there are fewer of them every day.

As a high school teacher, I was struck not only by how few students thought of them-selves as capable of singing, but how popular lip-synching to recorded music was. If there was any so-called singing at a talent show, it was most likely this silent semiventriloquism. Accompanied by air-guitar. Mimic music. Not the real thing. On hiking trips with adolescents, campfire singing consisted of parodied bits and pieces of songs from the radio and MTV. Without the record, the music died. They didn't even know any hymns from church. They didn't go to church.

Lest this seem like a things-ain't-what-they-used-to-be diatribe from someone with old-geezer tendencies, I insist that singing is as basic to being human as walking upright on two legs. And that if the professionals have taken it away for themselves, then it's time the amateurs took it back.

We don't even sing the national anthem anymore. That's left to some soloist out of the world of professional singers to do for us. It's a performance. One we do not join because we ain't got what it takes to sing.

As a nation, we can sing "Happy Birthday," "Jingle Bells," "America the Beautiful," "Three Blind Mice," and a few other nursery rhymes, and once a year stumble through something we can't even spell, much less sing well—"Old Hang Sign" is what it sounds like. And that's about it. Except for one other song, which may just be our real national anthem. Before I tell you its name, let me tell you how it came to be. Better yet, I'll tell you how to get to the very place where it was composed.

. . .

Fly to St. Joseph, Missouri. Rent a car. Head due west on Highway 36 for about two hundred miles across Kansas until you reach the little town of Athol in the Solomon River Valley. Ask directions to the farm of Pete and Ellen Rust. It's one mile further west, eight miles north and three fourths of a mile west again. The West Beaver Creek runs through the Rusts' farm, and near the headwaters of the creek, hidden in a grove of trees, is a rough log cabin. The Rusts are real nice people and will be glad to show you the cabin. In return, you should contribute to the fund to maintain and restore it. Because this is sacred ground—the headwaters of American song and the American psyche—what once was known as the western frontier.

I recommend that you sit alone on the grass in front of the cabin for a while. As did the man who built it 128 years ago. His journey was not unlike the one you've just made across the Great Plains of Kansas. He came here from Indiana in 1871, by foot and horseback, to this place just twenty miles from the geographic center of the United States. And he came alone. To get away and start over. Somewhere out West.

His first wife had died of plague, his second

from complications after childbirth, and his third wife from injuries suffered in an accident. His fourth marriage, made in haste to give his children a mother, was a bitter disaster. In his misery, he turned to alcohol, which seriously affected his capacity to carry out his life and work. In desperation, he sent his children to live with relatives in Illinois, and left his wife for a destination unknown.

The man who came this long way to build this tiny cabin so far from civilization was himself a civilized man. Well educated. A doctor. And not just an ordinary doctor, but a trained surgeon. Also a musician who sang and played the fiddle. He knew literature well enough to quote long passages from great books, and loved words well enough to write poetry. What he needed now was a place to put down roots and recover from sorrow and failure. He was looking for a place to call home.

He dug in here on his homestead a long way from anywhere, and built his cabin with his own hands. While he had indeed escaped from one set of troubles in Indiana, his new life had its own serious hardships. For all our romantic notions about the good life on the great American frontier, the Kansas plains were not paradise. Fierce cold, deep snow, wild winds in winter. Fierce heat, deep dust, and tornadoes in summer. Creeks and rivers that flooded in spring. Prairie fires, rattlesnakes, plagues of grasshoppers, and a mysterious equine disease that wiped out half of the horse population. The Native American Indians were fighting a last-ditch battle for their way of life, and often gave no quarter in their desperation. Then there were all the problems of distance from supplies, and distance from help in time of need. Hard place to make a go of a new life.

Worse if one had a serious alcohol problem, as did this man. Tough, too, if one got called out in the worst weather to ride long miles to amputate gangrenous feet or dig bullets and arrows out of patients who had no means to pay for the services of a surgeon.

Brewster M. Higley VII, M.D., was his name.

Despite the hardships of his life, he found time to sit on a stump in the sunshine—in front of his cabin in the silence of that place—and write poetry. About open country, clear skies, and the great joy of feeling at home at last. He was not one of those whom adversity destroys. Rather one of those whose virtues and strengths are catalyzed by tough times. Brewster Higley was one of those who would sing in hell itself.

One fall he wrote down some verses about his sense of well-being, filed them away between the pages of a book, and forgot about them. In the spring, a patient who had come to his cabin browsed through the doctor's books as he was being treated, found the poem, read it aloud, and urged the doctor to get it set to music.

Doc Higley took his patient's advice and carried the poem with him to Smith Center, Kansas, to share with his young friend Dan Kelly, the local druggist. Kelly had been a bugler in the Civil War, played several other musical instruments, and liked to compose songs. He took the doctor's poem with him that night when he went to see his girlfriend, Lula Harlan. They sat together on the couch and made music together. Lula's two brothers, Clarence and Eugene, joined in with fiddle and guitar. Before long, a song was born.

If you could be transported across time and space to the Harlans' home one Friday night in April 1873, in Smith Center, Kansas, you could join right in with the premier performance of the new song. They called it "My Western Home." But you would know it was "Home on the Range." And you would probably sing your lungs out, because if there's one song you likely know by heart, this is it. "Home on the Range" is our *real* national anthem. Frederick Jackson Turner would agree. His whole frontier theory of American history is summarized in the spirit of that song.

The song is larger than that, however. Millions and millions of people all over the world can sing it with you. People who have never seen Kansas or buffalo or deer or antelope. But who understand what the word *home* means and who are tired of discouraging words and who yearn for clear blue sky and a fine day away from the endless traffic of our lives.

Brewster M. Higley VII, M.D., moved on from Kansas in time because of age and health. Ever the optimist, he married again and lived happily with his wife Sarah Ellen. She was the home he had been looking for. When she was sixty-seven and he was in his ninetieth year, she passed away. He followed not long after. Died of grief, his family said. They are buried side by side in the final peace and quiet of a small cemetery in Shawnee, Oklahoma. "Where seldom is heard a discouraging word, and the skies are not cloudy all day."

*J*ewish, I'm not. But I often observe the spirit of Rosh Hashanah, the Jewish New Year. Not as Jews usually celebrate—not in a synagogue—and not for ten days. In my own way and time. The temper of Rosh Hashanah appeals to me. The idea of the new year coming in the fall fits my life better than January. During all the years I worked as a teacher and minister, the fall was the beginning of my annual cycle—the end of summer vacation and the start of work anew. That mind-set continues. By January, I am already in the middle of a cycle of living.

The ten days of the Jewish New Year, called the "Days of Awe," begin with the "Day of

119

Remembrance," and end with Yom Kippur, the "Day of Atonement." A trumpet made from a ram's horn is blown, summoning the people for judgment and self-assessment, for repentance and self-improvement. At the center of this event is a sense of hope. One gets personal accounts squared away so that one may go on with life, with high expectations for another year—a better year—to come. And someday, next year perhaps, Jerusalem—the City of God on Earth, with the Anointed One, the Messiah—will truly come. That is how the Jews see it and believe it.

This year on Rosh Hashanah, I stood out on the end of a high ridge in southeastern Utah and watched the sun go blazing down in a clear sky. September 19. No congregation, no horns, no hymns or prayers or candles. Just the passing of the daylight and the coming of night. Great silence. And a view of 60 million light-years when I looked straight up into the stars. "Days of Awe" indeed.

On occasion, in years past, I planted daffodil bulbs on Rosh Hashanah, as a reminder to myself that hope for better times is not enough—that one must be an active participant in the quality of the future. If I want flowers in the future, the planting must be done now.

One year I went so far as to plant an apple

tree and some strawberry starts, knowing full well that I would not see flowers or fruit for a long time to come. But I intended being there. Hope and faith must be active verbs.

My friend Willy and his six-year-old daughter, Emily, planted bulbs last week. Went to the seed store, bought a sack full of hardy crocus and a bulb-planting tool. Then they walked around their neighborhood and planted crocus bulbs in yards along the routes they take as they walk to the grocery store, to Emily's school, and the nearby playground. Places that needed a bulb or two. At the moment, Emily thinks of this as one more game her daddy plays with her. Willy thinks of it as "affirmative vandalism."

For five years in a row my two sons and I were right there in line when the local amusement park opened in the spring. This was a long time ago. We rode everything that moved— the Zipper, Matterhorn, Wild Mouse, Galaxie, bumper cars, and the Ferris wheel. Ate cotton candy, hot dogs, snow cones, candy apples, caramel corn, slurpies, licorice whips, and corn dogs. Our attitude was if you are going to get sick anyhow, you might as well go ahead and get really sick. It's a philosophy of life—go whole hog and take the consequences.

The boys are men now and married and

they work for a living—too old for this kid stuff. But I have started going again, now that I am younger than they are. My wife says I am looking for my childhood. So? Maybe I'll find it. I've tried being an adult. I know what that's like. Don't push me to choose.

Not that I've started doing the rides again or eating all the goop again. I've learned a few things, and besides, I'm waiting for the senior-citizen discounts and saving my strength for when my grandchildren are ready.

I go now simply because the amusement park is on my way when I walk to work. And I stop and watch. When you think about it and look at this activity dispassionately, human intelligence is called into question. Why is it that people will pay a dollar to have the hell scared out of them, knowing full well they will likely toss their cookies before it's over? And do it again and again and again. Why did my sons and I go year after year in springtime?

It had something to do with risk-taking. Wildness. Adventure. Wanting to break loose from being earthbound, but safely. Wanting the adrenaline to pump through us in that way that drives home the fact of life and death for a moment. Fear and release. All that, I guess. We didn't consciously think of it in that way, but those words point at what we not only wanted, but needed, to happen.

The rising of the sap in all living things in spring.

I know that I always went back to the more mundane tasks of life with a lighter heart, feeling a little braver, and loving being alive a little more.

I carry a permanent burst of excitement somewhere in my soul as my sons and I soar up and over the top of the Ferris wheel, the seat swinging free, the music playing, and us screaming YAAAAAgggh . . . as we fall through the air. The sky is blue. The sun is shining. Everything is green and alive and blooming. And so are we.

For that moment, *we are spring.*

In the same way that Native American Indians think about doing a rain dance. They are not just dancing *about* rain—they are *raining.* We weren't just observing spring, we were being spring. Anthropologists call this "participatory mana." The Indians call this the Way of Life.

In my hometown, in my childhood days, Easter Sunday was observed with a sunrise service. A great host of Baptists, about half of Waco, would rise before daybreak, dress in new clothes, and journey out to the local cemetery. Facing east, they would greet the rising sun with hymns and prayers. The belief was that Jesus, the Messiah, would return from the east, and raise up both the living and the dead together into heaven. And they didn't want to miss it.

My theology wasn't too clear then—and for that matter, it's still not too clear. But I do remember with clarity the power of the moment when people would sing "Up from the Grave He Arose" and the sun would suddenly come up and I would think I was going to fly away to heaven. It never happened. Year after year, nothing came but the sun. No angel choirs and no Saviors. None of my mother's explanations stemmed my disappointment. We went out there even on Easter Sundays when it was pouring down rain and we couldn't even see the sunrise. This confirmed my feeling that the whole thing was a hoax. I knew Jesus wouldn't come when it was raining.

Watching the sun rise—or the earth turn toward the sun—is mostly accidental now. Something that happens while on my way to do something else. Something I glance at when I'm up running for exercise and too busy to stop to look at. I don't think I'd get very far if I tried to organize a group of friends to get dressed up in new clothes and watch the sunrise in a graveyard on Easter or any other Sunday. This is for romantics, insomniacs, Sunday painters, and religious fanatics. And who has time these days to be one, even if one is one? But there's something missing when there's no Sabbath act of any kind in my life. No Rosh Hoshanah, no Easter sunrise. Not even much of a Sunday anymore. We live in a world where it is thought great progress that stores are open twenty-four hours a day, seven days a week, and it is a sign of great entrepreneurial industry to work on weekends. I need more than a read through the Sunday paper to feel I've experienced a Sabbath ritual. If I don't have time to live my life well the first time, when am I going to find the time to go back and live it over?

I know. I could go to church. But I went to church every Sunday for almost fifty years. And there are Sabbath moments I need that don't happen sitting in a pew.

Makes me think about a lady I know. She went to see a psychiatrist about her troubles. After listening to her, he wrote a prescription. He asked that she promise not to return until she had used up the prescription. When the druggist read the prescription, he returned it to her. "I can't fill this," he said, "but you can." The prescription: "Spend one hour some Sunday watching the sunrise while walking in a cemetery."

She did. She got in touch with the big picture again. It was the first time she had been to church in years. She goes several times a year, now. She won't go to heaven because of this. But her life on earth is no longer the hell it was.

Not far from the Tokyo International Airport is Naritasan, a Shingon sect Buddhist temple of great age and size. It is dedicated to Fudo-Myo-o, the deity of "Immovable Wisdom." More than 15 million people come to this shrine each year. On the grounds is a sub-temple containing a complete collection of Buddhist scriptures. The scriptures are housed in a round, ten-foot-tall structure, which is mounted on a base that turns. From the base of the wheel radiate long open spokes, somewhat like a Western turnstile. It is customary for a visitor to the temple to stand behind one of the spokes and turn the scriptures around once. You have to push hard, for it is very heavy. Slowly it turns, as you slowly consider the basic truths of Buddhism.

There is a bell to ring to call your deed to the attention of the gods.

Afterward, you write your troubles on a

piece of paper, fold the paper, and leave it hanging on a wood-and-bamboo fence. In time the rain and wind and sun will dispose of your page of troubles.

Buddhist, I'm not. Also not Japanese. But on two different occasions I have visited Narita-san on my way from something to somewhere, and have paused to turn the great wheel and leave my troubles on the fence. There are no words for these ritual moments and no reasons that words satisfy. It is a touching base with elemental needs. A finite gesture toward infinite concerns.

January 1 of 1990. Nagano-shi, Japan. Zenkoji Temple. Kondo Hall, the largest wooden building with a thatched roof in all of Japan. Thirty meters high, with a floor space of 1,766 square meters. Huge. The Japanese equivalent of the great Gothic cathedral of Chartres in France.

Inside it, in the inner sanctuary area of the high altar, the Amida Trinity is enshrined. (Amida Buddha, with Kannon and Daiseishi bodhisattvas on either side.) To the right side of the sanctuary is a stairway entrance to a long, pitch-dark, circular corridor underneath the high altar. Somewhere in this corridor is a lock hung on the wall. If, while groping your way in the dark through this circular corridor, you are fortunate enough to touch this lock, you are destined to go to the Buddhist paradise. Or so it is said.

So there I was on January 1. Groping my way along in the darkness and towing my wife along behind me by the hand. (She is afraid of the dark. I am also afraid of the dark, but she doesn't know that and she thinks as long as she holds my hand she will be okay. Family myths.) Anyhow, we're stumbling along in this wooden tunnel and it is seriously dark in here.

Feeling the walls and ceiling and floor for the lock. I am going to find this lock. But I am looking for a Western lock—something I can put my hand on. No luck. But I push on through the darkness and back into the light, with relief and also with the suspicion that there wasn't a lock down there in the first place. Somebody else must have found it and taken it with him. I braved the dark and didn't find a thing.

I asked a priest about this. He gave me his kindest smile. "Perhaps you were not looking in the correct way for the right thing. This is a rite of passage. You see, the corridor itself is the lock, representing a year of life. To unlock it means to have made the journey through the darkness with courage to the light. Happy New Year."

One reason I hang around with my friend Grady is because I like to watch him put on his shoes and socks. We work out together at a gym, and after we shower off and are getting dressed, the high point of the event comes. When Grady does his shoe-and-sock performance. He carefully examines each sock, trying to decide which one he wore last on which foot so he can reverse them now and put them on opposite feet so he doesn't wear out the big-toe side. He also turns them inside out to even the wear on both sides of the sock. I'm not kidding. This is a complicated ritual, not easily carried out—I know, I tried it once when Grady wasn't around.

When Grady has his socks repositioned correctly, he then puts one sock and one shoe on one foot—all the way to tying the laces. Followed by the other sock and other shoe. I observe that most people put on both socks and then both shoes. Sock, sock, shoe, shoe is the usual order. Grady is a sock, shoe, sock, shoe kind of guy. I've never talked to him about this. He might have a reason—a long reason—and I don't think I want to know.

Grady and I have played poker together for years—couple of hundred years or more. Well, no, it hasn't really been that long, but his name isn't Grady, either. His name ought to be Grady. Do you know people like that? People who got the wrong name when they were born. This guy is a Grady if I ever saw one, and I'll leave it at that. And when I say I've been playing poker with Grady for a couple of hundred years, it's because he's one of those guys who can take FOR-BLOODY-EVER deciding what to do with a hand. If you're dealing draw poker and you asked him how many cards he wants, you could go out for a full-course Chinese dinner and come back and he'd not only still be thinking, he wouldn't have noticed you left. Grady does not ever leap to conclusions.

But this isn't about Grady's poker playing.

It's about two gallons of yellow paint and the meaning of Grady's life.

Grady has a problem with scale. Scale in the sense of the real world being the base reference and a road map being drawn on a scale of one inch equals twenty miles. Like that. He tries to live on more than one scale at a time. In the real world and on the map at the same time. In the present and in the future at the same time. I will elaborate.

(In passing, I should point out that Grady is intelligent—he's got several diplomas from upmarket private colleges hanging on his wall to prove it. But being intelligent doesn't mean you aren't stupid. His income is good, too. It's his outgo that gets him in trouble.)

Anyhow, about the paint.

It all began seven years ago when Grady moved out of his marriage and out of his house, and into a bachelor apartment. Temporarily, or so he said. The apartment was a hole—in an old building that had once been pretty classy, but that was now dark, moldy, and depressing. The smell of stale bacon grease pretty well established the ambience of the building. He's been temporarily there for seven years. Grady says he's waiting for the future to clarify itself enough so that he can either fix up his present apartment, move into a better set of digs, or maybe move back home with his wife and family. Which is a real laugh because his wife divorced him, remarried, sold the old house, and moved to Wyoming five years ago. She is out of it, free and clear. There is some real lunatic optimism loose in Grady's head, because he still doesn't quite believe she's gone and it's all over. Grady doesn't come to hasty conclusions.

He's lived in this crummy apartment for seven years, and for every minute of that seven years he has been down and out about how awful the apartment makes him feel. He hates to come home to it at night. Says it's so ugly in there. His friends agree. Nobody goes over to Grady's house unless he wants to be depressed.

The walls are gray. The rug is gray. The drapes are gray. So's the furniture. He ought to at least paint the walls. He even knows what color. Yellow. Two gallons would do the living room, easy. It would be a start. And that's the heart of the problem.

See, if he painted the walls, the furniture wouldn't look good in there and he'd have to have new furniture, which means going shopping, and he doesn't have time to go shopping, and interior decorators are too opinionated and trendy, so he doesn't want one of those, and besides if he is going to buy new furniture, he might as well move on up to a better apartment.

But the kind of apartment he wants is expensive and he'd have to sign a lease and change his phone number and have his stationery reprinted. And if he is going to go to all that trouble and expense, he might as well buy a house, because real estate is going up and up and why wait until he can't afford it?

But buying takes so much time and is such a hassle what with real estate agents and banks and credit checks and all that. Besides, what if he falls in love in the meantime and she doesn't like the house, or maybe she would want kids and there he'd be owning a house in a neighborhood where the schools are not good, which would mean all the expense of private schools for the children.

Or, who knows, his wife may finally decide she made a big mistake in leaving him and would want to come back and there he would be with a house his wife wouldn't want and still having to pay private-school tuition for the children of his second marriage. He'd need a therapist before long, and everybody knows what they cost.

Grady figures a couple of gallons of paint could cost half a million dollars in the long run, and who needs that?

And I agree. It's a risk, I tell him. When the

sun finally starts to die and gets so hot it turns the surface of the earth into boiling rock, his new house will burn down, and he will regret all the time and trouble gone to waste, and his insurance money and the deposit money on the nonexistent children's nonexistent private school will be down the drain to boot. In between there will be carpenter ants, inflation, depression, famine, floods, earthquakes, mold, athlete's foot, and entropy. Painting his apartment living room yellow could lead to the end of the world. Grady seems comforted by the depth of my comprehension of the problem.

"Grady," says I, "you should turn yourself in to the Humane Society, and if nobody claims you in a couple of weeks, they will put you to sleep. It's the only way out. Because you are too dumb to live."

Grady's stuck. And he thinks getting unstuck and coming unglued are the same thing.

Grady also has this scale problem. Trying to live in several different time frameworks at the same time. He's trying to live today and tomorrow and next week and next year and next decade and next century all at once. And trying to live in his apartment now and in houses yet to come. I tell him he should just buy himself a cemetery plot now, dig a hole in it and pitch a tent over it, and move in. Save all that hassle in between.

So we had enough—Grady's friends. Enough of his being stuck straddling the present and the future. Enough of his moaning and groaning. It was casting a pall over poker games. We decided to shove him headlong into the perils of the next phase of his miserable existence. While he was off skiing one weekend, we bought the lousy paint and repainted his crummy living room. Hauled half his furniture to the Goodwill, had his rug shampooed, the windows washed, and bought him a potted plant and one goldfish in a bowl so that something alive was in there with him at night.

Oh, he appreciated the gesture all right. He even cried about it. Took us all out to dinner and made a great fuss. But he's not happy.

It's the paint. The paint's the wrong color. We used medium yellow. Lighter yellow was what he had in mind. And now if he repaints it, he will hurt our feelings, and if he doesn't, he'll go crazy living with that yellow, so Grady's stuck again.

We sent his ex-wife a sympathy card.

And sent Grady a bill for the damned paint.

The only reason I still hang out with him has to do with getting some new curtains in our house. You know what getting new curtains means. Grady's one of the few people I know to talk to about what getting new curtains can lead to. In fact, we may form a club called the Damned If You Do and Damned If You Don't Society of America. A subsection of the Fellowship of the Fridge. We'd probably never get a membership going. Most of our kind of folks wouldn't be able to make up their minds whether to join or just wait and see.

"*D*o you believe in God, Mr. Fulghum?" (The journalist interviewing me has shifted scale suddenly from the details of dailiness to the definition of the Divine.)

"No, but I do believe in Howard."

"Howard? You believe in Howard?"

"It all has to do with my mother's maiden name."

"Your mother's maiden name . . ."

"Was Howard. She came from a big Memphis clan that was pretty close and was referred to as the Howard Family. As a small child, I thought of myself as a member of the Howard Family because it was often an item of conversation as in 'The Howard Family is getting together,' and 'The Howard Family thinks people should write letters to their grandmother.' The matriarch, my grandmother, was referred to as Mother Howard."

"And you thought . . . she . . . was . . . God?"

"No, no. I just wanted you to first know how it was that Howard was a name that was important to me from early on in my life. What happened was that I got packed off to Sunday School at around age four and the first thing I learned was the Lord's Prayer, which begins 'Our Father, which art in heaven, Hallowed be Thy name.' And what I heard was, 'Our Father, which art in heaven, HOWARD be Thy name.' And since little kids tend to mutter prayers anyhow, nobody realized what I was saying, so I went right on believing that God's name was Howard. And believing I was a member of His family—the Howards. Since I was told that my grandfather had died and gone to heaven, God and my grandfather got all mixed up in my mind as one and the same. Which meant that I had a pretty comfy notion about God. When I knelt beside my bed each night and prayed, 'Our Father, which art in heaven, Howard be Thy name,' I thought about my grandfather and what a big shot he was because, of course, the prayer ends with 'For Thine is the kingdom, the power, and the glory forever and ever. Amen.' I went to bed feeling pretty well connected to the universe for a long, long time. It was a Howard Family Enterprise."

"You're not putting me on, are you?"

"Not at all. All human images of the ultimate ground of being are metaphors, and as metaphors go, this is a pretty homey one. And I thought it for so long that even when I passed through all those growing-up stages of skepticism, disbelief, revision, and confusion—somewhere in my mind I still believed in Howard. Because at the heart of that childhood image there is no alienation. I *belonged* to the whole big scheme of things. I lived and worked and had my being in the family store."

"So. Do you still believe in . . . Howard?"

"I'll give you what may seem to be an enigmatic evasion, but it's truly the only answer I have to your question. It's a line from the writings of a thirteenth-century Christian mystic. Meister Eckhart. 'The eye with which I see God is the very same eye with which God sees me.' That's what I believe."

"Does that mean that you are God?"

"Yes and no. It depends. In some cultures if a man says, 'I am God,' he will get shunned or even locked up as crazy. In some other cultures if a man says, 'I am God,' people will say, 'What took you so long to find out?' If you say you pray and talk to God, we will think of you as religious. If you say God talks to you, we will think of you as loony."

"I'm not sure I understand."

"Consider it this way. It makes a big difference if you think of God as transcendent or immanent; as up there somewhere or present here."

"Yes."

"Howard is a transcendent image of God. The God of childhood. The man in the long white beard on the throne in heaven—up there, somewhere else, separate from us . . . transcendent. On the other hand, if God is immanent, then there is no place God is not, and I am not separate from God. Hence, 'The eye with which I see God is the very same eye with which God sees me.' No boundaries between God and me."

There was a long silence between us. The journalist smiled. I smiled. She changed the subject. None of this discussion about Howard appeared in her article. I understand. Some things are hard to write about . . . hard to think about . . . hard to sort out. Maybe when she asked the first question, I should have just said, "Yes." As a favor to her. But the truth is I haven't finished thinking about God, and the God of my childhood and the God of my middle age are mixed in with the God of the wisdom that may yet come to me in my later years. Howard would understand.

On a long flight from Melbourne to Athens, an Australian carpenter, an Indian college professor in hydrology, and I had a memorable late-night theological discussion. The three of us were seated in one row, and the subject of God came up because our meals were accompanied by a little card on which was printed a short prayer of thanksgiving.

The professor made some remarks about *not* being thankful to *any* of the gods for this particular food. The carpenter composed a prayer of complaint. And the discussion was off and running.

The carpenter declared his theology had a lot to do with fleas and a dog.

Arguing whether or not a God exists is like fleas arguing whether or not the dog exists. Arguing over the correct name of God is like fleas arguing over the name of the dog. And arguing over whose notion of God is correct is like fleas arguing over who owns the dog.

We three ate our meal in silence for a while—digesting the godforsaken meal and the Australian version of theological Truth.

. . .

Later on, the Indian professor and I stood in the forward alcove of the 747 where the galley and rest rooms are, comparing the route map with what we could see out the porthole in the door.

Across Australia, Indonesia, to Singapore; across Malaysia, India, Pakistan, Saudi Arabia, and into Athens. Much of what we crossed was ocean.

Theology again. The Indian professor of hydrology this time. Hydrology is "the scientific study of the properties, distribution, and effects of water in the atmosphere, on the earth's surface, and in soil and rocks." He had this printed on his business card since he always had to explain about hydrology. In sum, a water expert.

He noted that we had just left a country where people worshiped the sun—on the beach with most or all of their clothes removed. And we were flying over countries whose people believed it was the will of Allah that women should be completely covered, even on beaches. The name of God varied from country to country; the holy book was not the same; the rituals and dogmas and routes to heaven were not the same. And so certain were the followers of the different religions of their rectitude, they would gladly war with one another—kill each other—to have their beliefs and metaphors prevail. Yet in this same plane, flying peacefully along, are these same people.

Clearly this troubled the professor—grieved him.

He shook his head and asked why this must be so. Why? Why?

The professor pointed out the Indian Ocean beneath us at the moment.

He spoke of water, his specialty.

"Water is everywhere and in all living things—we cannot be separated from water. No water, no life. Period. Water comes in many forms—liquid, vapor, ice, snow, fog, rain, hail. But no matter the form, it's still water.

"Human beings give this stuff many names in many languages, in all its forms. It's crazy to argue over what its true name is. Call it what you will, there is no difference to the water. It is what it is.

"Human beings drink water from many vessels—cups, glasses, jugs, skins, their own hands, whatever. To argue about which container is proper for the water is crazy. The container doesn't change the water.

"Some like it hot, some like it cold, some like it iced, some fizzy, some with stuff mixed in with it—alcohol, coffee, whatever. No matter. It does not change the nature of the water.

"Never mind the name or the cup or the mix. These are not important.

"What we have in common is thirst. Thirst!

"Thirst for the water of Life!"

As it is with water, so is it with God.

"I don't know much about God," said the professor of hydrology. "All I know is water. And that we are momentary waves in some great everlasting ocean, and the waves and the water are one."

He poured us each a paper cup full of water and we drank.

Emily, five, has become a grace fanatic. Or, in her own terms, "a great amenner."

Though her family is not particularly religious and has not previously had a tradition of prayer before meals, Emily is now committed to the custom. Her father, my friend Willy, isn't sure where she got the idea, but the family doesn't want to squash rectitude in their youngest child. So they dutifully hold hands and bow heads at dinnertime while Emily, the high priestess of her own sacred mystery cult, holds forth in prayer:

Hello. This is Emily. I'm fine, how are you?

Thanks for the sky and birds and stuff.

Actually, I'm having a pretty good week.

And thanks for the mashed potatoes, but not for the lima beans.

I thank you really much for the meatloaf.

And thanks for the chairs, and the tables, and the doors, and the couch and the television and the walls and the roof and the bed and the bathroom and the towels and the grass and the clouds and the street and . . .

(By now her eight-year-old brother, who says his prayers in private, is beginning to grit his teeth and roll his eyes into the back of his head as he endures what he thinks is a shameless shuck on Emily's part—and Emily knows she'd better shut up now or she will suffer later, so she ends.)

"Take care. Amen, from Emily."

Her parents think of this daily vesper as the Emily Report. She's found a way to get her family to sit still and listen to her—something that doesn't happen too much during the daily traffic of family life.

As she prays, her father peeks at his five-year-old. He wants to be sure he sees her. He wants to remember his youngest child like this—as she heads out the door of innocence into the world-as-it-is. He wants to be there as she makes her announcement of self to the mystery of existence.

These times of quiet grace calm his spirit. Unlike Emily's brother, her father is in no hurry to have the prayer end. These times go by once and all too quickly.

Hello. This is Emily. It's a good day
   here, after all.
I'm really sorry for what I did and I
   won't ever do it again.
Please help Poppy. Thanks for dogs
   and cats.
Thanks, again, for more mashed
   potatoes.
Please try to do something about lima
   beans.
I really want to thank you especially for
   my birthday which is coming soon.
Thanks for friends. But not for people
   who are jerks [looking at her brother].
Take care and keep in touch. Amen.
   From Emily.

Sometime soon I should tell Emily about Howard.

Howard is Emily's kind of guy. And vice versa.

In my childhood I was told that God was all-powerful and lived far, far away. And that I could not see Him until after I died. When I asked why, if God was so powerful, there were children starving in Mexico, I was told it was the will of God and that I should not worry about it. Instead, I should be concerned about making sure I didn't attend the upcoming high school prom, because dancing was a sin and I should try not to sin.

Now I am older. And I know that God is everywhere and in all things. There is nowhere that God is not, even in me. I also know that starving comes from not having enough food, and that is a human problem about which something can be done.

I know now that dancing comes from having much joy.

And when everyone has enough to eat, everyone will dance, especially Howard.

It took me fifty years to figure that out.

Pass it on. Come to the dance.

*I*n the summer of 1959. At the Feather River Inn near the town of Blairsden in the Sierra Nevada Mountains of northern California. A resort environment. And I, just out of college, have a job that combines being the night desk clerk in the lodge and helping out with the horse-wrangling at the stables. The owner/manager is Italian-Swiss, with European notions about conditions of employment. He and I do not get along. I think he's a fascist who wants peasant employees who know their place, and he thinks I'm a good example of how democracy can be carried too far. I'm twenty-two and pretty free with my opinions, and he's fifty-two and has a few opinions of his own.

One week the employees had been served the same thing for lunch every single day. Two wieners, a mound of sauerkraut, and stale rolls. To compound insult with injury, the cost of meals was deducted from our check. I was outraged.

On Friday night of that awful week, I was at my desk job around 11:00 P.M., and the night auditor had just come on duty. I went into the kitchen to get a bite to eat and saw notes to the chef to the effect that wieners and sauerkraut are on the employee menu for two more days.

That tears it. I quit! For lack of any better audience, I unloaded on the night auditor, Sigmund Wollman. I declared that I have had it up to here; that I am going to get a plate of wieners and sauerkraut and go and wake up the owner and throw it on him. I am sick and tired of this crap and insulted and nobody is going to make me eat wieners and sauerkraut for a whole week and make me pay for it and who does he think he is anyhow and how can life be sustained on wieners and sauerkraut and this is un-American and I don't like wieners and sauerkraut enough to eat it one day for God's sake and the whole hotel stinks anyhow and the horses are all nags and the guests are all idiots and I'm packing my bags and heading for Montana where they never even heard of wieners and sauerkraut and wouldn't feed that stuff to pigs. Something like that. I'm still mad about it.

I raved on in this way for twenty minutes, and needn't repeat it all here. You get the drift. My monologue was delivered at the top of my lungs, punctuated by blows on the front desk with a flyswatter, the kicking of chairs, and much profanity. A call to arms, freedom, un-ions, uprisings, and the breaking of chains for the working masses.

As I pitched my fit, Sigmund Wollman, the night auditor, sat quietly on his stool, smoking a cigarette, watching me with sorrowful eyes. Put a bloodhound in a suit and tie and you have Sigmund Wollman. He's got good reason to look sorrowful. Survivor of Auschwitz. Three years. German Jew. Thin, coughed a lot. He liked being alone at the night job—gave him intellectual space, gave him peace and quiet, and, even more, he could go into the kitchen and have a snack whenever he wanted to—all the wieners and sauerkraut he wanted. To him, a feast. More than that, there's nobody around at night to tell him what to do. In Auschwitz he dreamed of such a time. The only person he sees at work is me, the nightly disturber of his dream. Our shifts overlap for an hour. And here I am again. A one-man war party at full cry.

"Fulchum, are you finished?"

"No. Why?"

"Lissen, Fulchum. Lissen me, lissen me. You know what's wrong with you? It's not wieners and kraut and it's not the boss and it's not the chef and it's not this job."

"So what's wrong with me?"

"Fulchum, you think you know everything, but you don't know the difference between an inconvenience and a problem.

"If you break your neck, if you have nothing to eat, if your house is on fire—then you got a problem. Everything else is inconvenience. Life *is* inconvenient. Life *is* lumpy.

"Learn to separate the inconveniences from the real problems. You will live longer. And will not annoy people like me so much. Good night."

In a gesture combining dismissal and blessing, he waved me off to bed.

Seldom in my life have I been hit between the eyes with truth so hard. Years later I heard a Japanese Zen Buddhist priest describe what the moment of enlightenment was like and I knew exactly what he meant. There in that late-night darkness of the Feather River Inn,

Sigmund Wollman simultaneously kicked my butt and opened a window in my mind.

For thirty years now, in times of stress and strain, when something has me backed against the wall and I'm ready to do something really stupid with my anger, a sorrowful face appears in my mind and asks: "Fulchum. Problem or inconvenience?"

I think of this as the Wollman Test of Reality. Life is lumpy. And a lump in the oatmeal, a lump in the throat, and a lump in a breast are not the same lump. One should learn the difference. Good night, Sig.

A houseboat on our dock was sold, and since we have a "no dogs" rule and the new owners had a dog, the possibility of social conflict was high. However, with unexpected care and sensitivity, the couple went from door to door explaining that they understood the rule, but theirs was a very old, very well-behaved dog that did not bark and spent most of the time inside. Besides being old, the dog was not in good health and would probably die soon. They wanted permission to have the dog on the dock for a try-it-and-see reality check. The alternative was to have the dog put away. If the dock tenants voted thumbs-down on the dog, then the dog owners would do what had to be done.

Now I'm afraid of dogs, if you want to know the truth. Seriously afraid. Having been chewed up by big dogs twice as a child, and having twice gone through the full rabies treatment, I am not enthusiastic about being around dogs.

But what am I supposed to say? "Too bad, lady, but you'll have to kill your dog."

Still, I don't care what they say about their pooch—all dog owners think their dog is an exceptional dog. Ha! I know all canines are hyenas at heart. But I can work around this problem—all I have to do is stay inside for a month and vote no, and the dog is out of my life.

So, here comes the dog.

Big dog. Half German shepherd and half Dalmatian. Stout, black-and-white lady dog.

Name is Gyda—a name you might expect for a blond Norwegian bank teller in a bikini on a beach in Spain—but not for a four-legged pet with bad breath.

During the trial month, as I was sitting on the deck of my houseboat each morning, she and her mistress would pass me on the way to the dog's morning walk-and-dump experience. When the pooch would see me, she would stop, sit down on the dock, cock her head, and look at me. No bark, no whine, no slobber. Just looking. Me? No dog had ever just sat and looked at me like this before. I felt the way an antelope must feel when a lion sits down and takes a look. Attack dogs do this just before they go for your throat.

In time, though, my fear turned to curiosity. What's with this dog?

Then curiosity became respect. What's with me?

One morning I reached out and petted her on the head.

I know people pet dogs all the time and it's no big deal, but if you were as afraid of dogs as I was (notice the past tense), then you'd know this was not an incidental moment. She let me pet her. No hand-licking, no jumping around and barking. Just a solemn acknowledgment of kindness received. With that touch, Gyda and I became connected somehow. Much to my wife's astonishment, I even invited Gyda over to our house as a personal guest on occasion. We sat together on the porch and watched ducks. My wife wanted to know what was going on, and I didn't want to talk about it. It's embarrassing to be wrong about something—humiliating to have to change my mind.

Sometimes I took Gyda along on walks. I

talked to her. Me, the man who thinks talking to dogs is dumb. Though she never barked or made a sound that I know of, she would stop and sit down and look at me while I talked. I once explained the difference between the music of B. B. King and Chuck Berry to her, and she never took her eyes off me. That's a cool dog.

The vote never came up on the dock. Gyda took us all in. Everybody had a personal relationship with her. I learned a lot about the power of keeping your mouth shut and your eyes open from that dog. She became a kind of silent great-aunt figure to us all. So she stayed and became a welcome part of daily life. We had needed a classy dog and didn't know it.

I'll tell you just how far things went. When her owners decided to get married and asked me to perform the wedding, I went along with the idea of Gyda somehow being part of the ceremony. Because she was, after all, her mistress's best friend.

If I could show you the video of the wedding, you'd see me, the minister, in my black gown, walking into the site of the ceremony in the park with a big old black-and-white dog at my side. The dog is wearing a huge white bow

around her neck—white because she was, as
far as anyone knows, a virgin. Truly, the maid
of honor.

Gyda had cancer all this time. Her mistress
went to the vet one morning with Gyda in her
arms and came back alone. I cried. The dock
was dressed in invisible crepe for a week.
Here's the notice I put in everyone's mailbox:

Nobody is more surprised than I to be
writing this. Everybody knows about me
and dogs. I avoid them when I can and
look upon their owners with sour suspicion. On the other hand, there was Gyda.
And there is Bob and Blair. Sometimes I
am wrong.

So I write to invite you to a memorial
service kind of occasion on Sunday morning, August 6. Coffee at 9, followed by a
celebration of a life well lived, followed by
a potluck brunch.

Gyda became a kind of symbol for the
best kinds of relationships that are possible in the close community on our dock—
and a symbol for the best kinds of relationships between living creatures in
general. Almost anything can be dealt
with if people are of good will and light

hearts and strong values. I believe that. Even a dog on the dock can work out. Gyda reminded me as she went by each day that what makes us rich here is not the escalating values of our floating homes, but the careful quality of our on-going relationships that somehow respect both individual rights and group needs. Gyda's coming increased our humanity in a funny but critical way. Gyda's departing leaves a hole in our daily lives. We were more generous to each other because of her.

I miss that dog. A lot.

We did indeed gather on that Sunday morning in August—thirty of us—and told stories that were as much about us as Gyda. Mostly about the attachments possible between living creatures when they are patient with one another. We buried her ashes under a rhododendron bush that's planted in a barrel on her owners' back porch. I always nod in her direction when I pass by.

Gyda. The grand old virgin aunt in the dog suit.

My seminary training didn't cover how to perform a dog funeral.

It takes a real dog to teach that. And when the pupil is ready, the teacher appears.

*T*he most time-bound man I know lives in my neighborhood. He's always in a hurry—and always late. Always harassed and fuzzed out. I'm not exactly sure just what he does for a living, but it seems to involve buying and selling something downtown. He's a business-man.

His choice of appropriate transportation for his coming and going is a brand-new Range Rover, a vehicle built by the British for high adventure. It is equally capable in steep canyons, quicksand, and blizzard conditions. It can outrun a lion and take a rhino charge head-on. This particular veldtmobile is equipped with a winch, a gun rack, and a CB radio, as well as an impressive stereo system, two cellular phones, a fax machine, and a coffee maker in the glove compartment.

Mostly my neighbor takes his Range Rover as far as downtown. So far it has faced the dangers of the underground parking ramps of the First National Bank, and the hostile natives at a car wash. As for animal encounters, rumor is he backed over either a cat or a squirrel. Maybe both.

Daily I see my neighbor rushing out of his house, burdened with the impedimenta of high adventure. Carrying golf bag, gym bag, lunch bag, raincoat, umbrella, coffee cup, a sack of garbage for the dumpster, and his briefcase. On the day I shall describe, he has two little pieces of bloody toilet paper stuck to his chin from a hasty encounter with his razor, and a knitted brow from a hasty encounter with his wife. So far, it has not been a good morning.

About the briefcase. It is made of the purest, unblemished belting leather, a quarter of an inch thick. The best part of the hides of four carefully selected cows, who gave their lives that he might carry this talisman of success. Solid-brass hardware, combination lock, lined with watered silk, and his name embossed in gold. By itself, empty, the briefcase weighs maybe ten pounds. Twenty pounds full. A heavy item in every sense of the word.

· · ·

So it's a Tuesday morning around seven o'-clock on a fine day in June. A neighbor lady and I hit the street headed for work about the same time. She's a social worker for the Episcopal Church and drives an eight-year-old Ford Just-Get-Me-There-and-Back-Please-God sedan. And I drive a 1952 GMC two-ton Go-Ahead-and-Hit-Me panel truck.

At the same time, the owner of the Range Rover rushes up. His life is leveraged to the max these days, and his mind is in three continents at once. Time is of the essence. He is in no mood to make small talk. He grunts at us as he loads his lorry for the expedition downtown, leaps into the front seat, and cranks the mighty engine in the spirit of a holder of a pole position at Indy.

Uh-oh—he has left his coffee cup and briefcase on the roof of the Range Rover, and there they remain as he rolls away.

To the rescue comes the nice lady social worker for the Episcopal Church in her old Ford. She chases after him, urgently honking her horn, which he ignores because he is already on his cellular phone talking to London. As a pin affects a swollen balloon, so does her unceasing honking affect his existential circumstance. He throws the phone to the floor of the car, leans out the window, and displays the middle finger of his left hand to the lady. But the lady is focused on her rescue mission and honks on while waving him to stop.

I, in the meantime, driving close behind as a kind of third float in this little parade, likewise try to get his attention. Mine is an "aaaoooo-gaah" horn salvaged out of an old Model A. The combination of "HONK, HONK, HONK" and "AAAOOOOGAAH, AAAOOOOGAAH, AAAOOOOGAAH" is too much. He jams on his brakes, flings open the door of the veldt-mobile, and tries to get out—without first un-latching his seat belt.

At the same moment, his morning cup of coffee slides off the roof, bounces across the hood, and smashes into the street.

Followed by his brassbound briefcase, which crashes onto the hood, scrapes across the paint with a fingernails-on-blackboard screech, and flops into the street on top of the broken coffee cup.

The dear lady, mission accomplished, coasts slowly around the scene of the acci-dent, smiles, waves, sings out "Have a nice day!" to her neighbor dangling from the car in the clutches of his seat belt.

And, no, she did not, as you might antici-pate, run over his briefcase.

No, she did not.
I did.

The nice lady social worker and I meant well.
It's not always easy or simple doing good.
When I told her later about the briefcase, she
grinned. None of us is pure. Did I run over it on
purpose? I don't know. As I say, none of us is
pure.

The owner of the veldtmobile is a little dis-
tant these days, though his wife smiles and
waves. I hear it cost him four hundred dollars
to have his hood and fender repaired and repainted. I see that he has a new briefcase.
Just exactly like the last one, but without coffee stains and street grit scratched into the
leather. In time, no doubt, the dust will settle,
and he will sort this out. He's not a bad guy.
Like me, he takes on more than he can handle
sometimes. Like me, he gets confused about
what's important. I see myself in his mirror. It's
less embarrassing to talk about how he runs
his life than to talk about the cartoon quality of
my own.

In the meantime, he's unhappy with us. I
hear he thinks we ruined his day.

And thinks we cost him money and time,
and kept him from getting his business done.

. . .

I think he may not know as much as he needs to know about the most basic business concern of all: profit and loss. Here's a very old profit-and-loss statement to put on the wall of his business and on the wall of mine:

"What does it profit a man if he gain the whole world and lose his own soul?"

*B*usiness magazines have been pointing out for some time that one of the fastest-growing investment opportunities is off-premise storage for the home-owning consumer. Store-it-yourself operations are expanding as fast as land can be found to build them. Because Americans are acquiring more stuff than they can pack into their homes and yards.

A conversation with the manager of one of these operations confirms this. "People got to have a place for the camper and the boat and the trail bikes and all the secondhand stuff they're saving to put in the summer place they haven't bought yet but will get soon, and for all the stuff they don't want around but don't want to give away because someday they might need it or else someday they are going to have a yard sale. There's also all the stuff they are going to fix someday but not now. So they come over here and rent themselves a mini-warehouse. Usually they start with a small space and then move on up to a bigger unit. Next thing you know, they need another unit. One guy who rents here has five. Fills one a year."

I was just looking for a place to put our furnishings while our houseboat gets overhauled. But there *is* a bunch of stuff I might just leave in storage when we move back in. I can relate to the manager's description. Sometimes I even answer my phone, "Fulghum's Moving and Storage," because I spend so much time hauling stuff from place to place because there's too much of it. Renting a miniware-house is better than burying the extra stuff in the backyard, or in my case, rowing out to deep water and dropping it over the side. What is this extra stuff? you ask. I don't want to talk about it. I don't *know* what most of it is—it's in boxes—and I don't *know* where I got it. Check *your* attic, basement, garage, or closets. *That* stuff. The stuff that just *happens.* The stuff that crawls into your life at night while you are asleep.

The manager of the ministorage went on to

say that his most interesting customer was a middle-aged guy who filled up one of the biggest storage units in one summer. His wife came the following spring with another station-wagon load of stuff, but there was no room left in the unit, and she drove away mad. The next day the guy showed up with a Goodwill truck following him and told the Goodwill crew to empty the unit clean, which they did. The man drove away with a contented look on his face.

A week later, the man came back with a La-Z-Boy reclining chair, a gooseneck lamp, and a side table. Also a box of cigars and a six-pack of Moosehead beer. He turned the storage unit into a kind of living room. About once a week, around six o'clock, the guy drops by with his evening paper and sits in solitude in the storage unit for a while.

The manager thinks this guy is a little strange.

Not me. I think he's sane and onto something big.

I rented the space next to him.

Maybe I'll catch what he's got.

Watch for the going-out-of-business sale at Fulghum's Moving and Storage.

And the opening of Fulghum's Ministorage Ashram and One-Man Tavern.

"Chinkelty-tink, chinkelty-tink, chinkelty-tinklety-tinklety-tink."

A sound from a street corner in Waco, Texas. In the late afternoon of a windy December day in 1944. Just in front of the Woolworth's five-and-dime store. A tall, slender, middle-aged man in suit, tie, overcoat, and Stetson hat stands by a red steel tripod from which hangs a black iron soup kettle. An eight-year-old kid, bundled up snugly against the cold, is with him, and is working up a little rhythm with a small bell. It is a privilege for the child to ring the bell. First time. An important promotion. For in previous years at this same post, it has been the prerogative of the man.

171

Admonished not to do anything silly, the kid is trying to mix a little joy in with the necessary solemnity required of one who has been trusted. "Chinkelty-tink, chinkelty-tink, chinkelty-tinklety-tinklety-tink." The kid is me. The man is my father. For an hour the two of us are the Salvation Army.

At dusk, as people started home from work, the real Salvation Army appeared. In proper uniforms. Dark blue with red piping. Carrying a flag with the words "Blood and Fire" on it. The Salvation Army Band, as well. Brass drum, tambourine, trumpet, French horn, trombone. I was allowed to ring along when they played "Jingle Bells." And allowed to occasionally shout, "Put a nickel on the drum! Please put a nickel on the drum!" between carols. What I really wanted to do most of all was play the big drum. And I would have played the drum—if only they had asked.

My father was not a Christian. At least not by the standards of the Salvation Army, the Baptist Church, or my mother. Oh, he went to church once in a while—Easter, Christmas, and Mother's Day. But he didn't have much use for the church crowd. Thought they were mostly Sunday talkers. Yet year after year he took me along with him to ring the bell for this army of God. Sometimes, I saw him quietly singing along with the hymns played by the band. He didn't sing in church—it surprised me to hear him sing here—and I didn't realize he knew all the words by heart. My father once told me if he was going to be a Christian, he would join the Salvation Army—they practiced what they preached.

He did join the Salvation Army temporarily— every year during the Christmas holidays, as one of the local businessmen who volunteered to tend the kettles. But there was a deeper reason for his participation. Years later, after my father died, his sister told me that when the family home had burned down, leaving the family destitute, the Salvation Army came to the rescue. My father was helped by the Salvation Army to find his first job. His debt to them was large. He owed. My aunt said that the family was so humiliated about their poverty that they never talked about it, even among themselves. All the help they got in that awful time was from the Salvation Army. I finally understood why I was ringing that bell.

"HELP! HELP! HELP THE POOR CHILDREN! THE POOR CHILDREN!"

A small child—a six-year-old blond urchin in dirty overalls, crusty sweater, ill-kempt hair, and house slippers is exhorting the shoppers at the entrance to a suburban shopping center. *"CHANGELDY, CHANGELDY, CHANGELDY!"* The brass bell he holds is rung with ferocious insistence as he points at the black plastic kettle hanging from the red plastic tripod. "IN THE POT!" he shouts, *"PLEASE PUT SOMETHING IN THE POT FOR THE BABY JEEZIS!"*

The child seems to be alone. About thirty feet away, however, there is a man keeping watch over him. Youngish man, well dressed—suit, tie, overcoat, Stetson hat. A rainy night in Seattle the week before Christmas 1969. The man is me. The kid is mine. Sam. Second son—the family dingdong.

Like my father and me at another time, my son and I are the Salvation Army for an evening, such as we are. Volunteers. Sam is not exactly wearing the standard army uniform, but I didn't dress him that way—it's his usual around-the-house getup. Professional urchin. Dickensian. Between his appearance and his enthusiasm, he is a dynamite fund-raiser. I just hand him the bell—say, "Sic'em, Sam," and get out of the way. Nobody turns him down.

Since there is no band, on occasion he will sing "Jingle Bells" in his most sincere little voice. People can't get their wallets out fast enough. More than once he has managed to fill the kettle completely. The Salvation Army officer who supervises us is really impressed. Told me they could use a few more like him. Not me. One of these is enough.

Here's a small sample of a typical nonstop inquiry from Sam, in the car riding home after kettle duty:

"If there is a Salvation Army, is there a Salvation Navy?"

"How about a Salvation Air Force? Are angels the Salvation Air Force?"

"How do you get in the Salvation Green Berets? And what do they do?"

"Do they have tanks? Do they really eat out of those kettles? Where do they keep their tanks? Can I have a ride in one of their tanks? Do they buy tanks with the money in the kettle? Do the Salvation Army Green Berets jump out of airplanes? Maybe the angels drop them? Where does the Salvation Army fight? Who do they fight? Are we going to have to fight? Does the Salvation Army have a bomb? Where do they keep it? Can we see it? How many tanks do you suppose they have? Do we belong to the Salvation Army?"

"Yes."

. . .

Like my father before me, I have reason to admire the Salvos. There are only about twenty-five thousand soldiers in this army, and they are thinly spread across eighty-six countries. Yet wherever there is trouble, there also is the Salvation Army. An army that takes no prisoners—an army whose only enemies are degradation, pain, and sorrow. As a parish minister engaged in the social concerns of my community, I found the Army at work wherever human need was greatest. Doing the hard stuff—the work nobody else would do. Shelters for the homeless, food for the hungry, refuge for the battered, company for the aged, and a hand to alcoholics, drug addicts, the jobless, the young. Whenever there was no other place to turn, the end of the road had someone from the Army beside it. The only qualification was need. No test of faith, race, color, sex, or place in life. Just need. As one officer explained to me, "Jesus was one of the homeless, you know."

Because I was a Unitarian, some Christian groups shunned me and my church. Not the Salvos. "If you want to help us help others, come on, and welcome," said the Salvation Army colonel when we offered. "We need help sorting out human problems here on earth; God will sort out the rest of the problems later."

And so for many years our little heathen Unitarian church kept the kettles boiling for the Salvation Army every December. They didn't quite know what to make of us, especially when we decided to form our own band.

A junior high school teacher of music offered to conduct what we called the Salvation *Smarmy* Band, and the word went out for volunteers. At least forty people turned up that first Sunday afternoon for rehearsal. About half those present were youngsters just starting out with an instrument. Their moms sent them. A few hotshot high school musicians gave some hope for an actual melody being carried by the band. The most enthusiastic recruits came from the ranks of the middle-aged men who had played in a band all the way through college and loved every minute of it. The good old days were still strong in their minds. Their lips were long gone, but they owned horns and came to play.

And who do you think played the bass drum? Me, that's who. Of course. If you are patient long enough, some dreams come true and fate will draft you.

To make a long, wonderfully ridiculous story short, the band actually showed up at the shopping center for their gig. The youngsters had found a bunch of World War II–vintage combat helmets to wear—it was an Army band, right? And the older guys wore Mexican Mariachi Band sombreros left over from a piñata party at church. And play? We played! I *mean* we *played*! Something powerful and mighty. Forty of us—hooting and honking away at full blast there on the sidewalk. The time of our lives! And people came from all over the shopping mall to see what on earth was going on.

Because my bass drum playing proved a little erratic, a lot of what we did sounded a little bit Brazilian. The "Hark the Herald Angels" mambo was my specialty. In B-flat major, my key.

What with all this din, and with my kid Sam clanging his bell and shouting "HELP, HELP, THE POOR CHILDREN," we were an unavoidable event. The Herald Angels had nothing on us. We Harked up a storm. And we raised so much money the kettle was filled to overflowing. A kettle record, actually.

The Salvation Army officer wouldn't show up to empty the kettle until we left. He was a little embarrassed, I think. But I saw him sitting out in the parking lot in his truck. Smiling. He was sincere when he said he would take any help he could get. We didn't play very long, anyhow. The old guys' lips blew out, and the moms came for the kids who had to get home to bed. *Sic transit gloria mundi.*

Several years have gone by since I tended kettle. Things have changed. The Salvation Army tries to hire the unemployed to ring the bell these days, and I'm not active in the church or in town much during the Christmas season, anyhow. It's easier to send a check in the mail. The kettles and tripods are plastic, and standing around shopping malls at Christmastime depresses me. I get upset at the lack of charity sometimes—the small change from people who could afford to and should put a whole lot more money in the pot. I sympathize with my son Sam's desire to run after people and hit them with the tambourine when they don't do their share.

But it does no good—solves nothing—to distance myself from the front lines of human need by using the mail as a safe shelter. I believe that serving the best ends of humanity means getting out in the middle of it just as it is, not staying home writing checks and thinking hopeful thoughts. The world does not need tourists who ride by in a bus clucking their tongues. The world as it is needs those who will love it enough to change it, with what they have, where they are. And you're damned right that's idealistic. No apology. When idealism goes into the trash as junk mail, we're finished.

In one way or another, I'm going back to kettle duty on the streets this year—literally or in some equivalent task. It will help the work of the Army, but it will also help me. I will have to stand still for a while and see the world as it goes by. As I have gone by. It will give me a chance to listen for the far-off sound of a bell rung by a child in front of the Woolworth's store in Waco, Texas, one winter's eve. To imagine my father standing beside me. To see his face. To hear the bell of another kid clanging away in the rainy Seattle night. To see his face. And to turn and look at the window glass in the storefront behind me and see my own reflection. If you see me, put something in the kettle. Be generous. I'd hate to have to hit you with the tambourine.

*F*unerals, American-style, are not supposed to be funny. Death must be treated with solemn dignity. Black clothing. Best serious face. Hushed tones. Slow movements. We are patient with the dead. Give the dead priority time. And speak of them with respect and reverence, deserved or not. This is our public protocol of funerals.

However. Like the careless shape of life itself, funerals often do not work out quite according to plan. As a parish minister involved backstage in more than two hundred funerals, I can testify that, like weddings, funerals have a soap-opera quality that can get out of hand and turn into comic operas worthy of Gilbert and Sullivan.

The following funeral story has a credibility problem. As you read along, you may begin to think I am making it up. In fact, I am making it *down.* As long as I had to change names and locations for the usual reasons, it seemed best to reduce the craziness and obscenity to a more believable size. If you think this version is wild, you should have been there when the real widow hit the fan.

A grandson of the deceased set the wheels in motion. The family patriarch had died. The religious mixture in the large family was so varied and volatile that a minister holding some neutral ground was required. A clergyman from out of town. Would I come? All the way from Seattle to a small town in Oregon? Since the grandson was a member of my church and a friend, I went.

The widow of the deceased, grandmother of the clan, was a lapsed Lutheran with a grudge against the local Lutheran minister. Furthermore, her first and truest love had checked out of their engagement to become a Catholic priest, leaving behind in his almost-bride a lifelong antagonism for the whole lot of what she referred to as "those gooses in the God Squad." The feeling was intensified when she found out her priest had eventually run off with a nun from a parish in St. Paul, Minnesota. If she ever got her hands on Father Olson, she would tear his heart out as he had hers. Grandma did not attend church. But she did pray. "I pray that Father Olson will burn in hell," she said.

As you may sense, the widowed grandma was looked upon by the town as a classic character. All the clichés applied—"heart of gold . . . big bark but not a bad bite . . . a lady at a party, but tough as nails in a fight and a little bit set in her ways . . . somewhat salty in her language."

The man she finally married, William Lefhart Hogaboom II, now deceased, was, in his own way, a churchgoing man. Except his "church" was the local post of the Veterans of Foreign Wars. And within its brotherhood, he was known more informally as Hogfart Hogaboom.

With the other young men of the town he had gone off to fight for liberty in France. The experiences they shared forged a lasting bond. He was a founding member of the local VFW post and spent more time there than he did at home. He rose through the ranks and held all the offices. He marched in parades, attended conventions, and lobbied for the VFW in Washington.

As the distance from the Great War increased, the VFW evolved into a private men's
club wherein the old guys gathered to play
dominoes, sip a little straight bourbon, smoke
cigars, tell lies, and hide out from their wives
and jobs. They occasionally hired a stripper
from San Francisco to raise their failing blood
pressure.

Now Old Lady Hogaboom had no more use
for the VFW than she did for churches and
clergymen. She thought her husband had
squandered his life at the VFW Hall, and she
was certain most of his buddies were not the
war heroes they claimed to be. "Veterans of
Foreign Women" is what she called them. So
when her husband died, she did not want the
VFW troop invited or involved when it came to
the funeral.

Now before we come to the funeral itself, here
are some background items you need to know
in order to have a full appreciation of what took
place at the cemetery:

1. The VFW had a drum-and-bugle corps, with
   a rifle-drill team. Rifles painted white. Helmets chrome-plated. Once they may have
   been a fairly sharp outfit on parade, but now
   they were old duffers who played off-key
   and marched out of step. Mostly they liked

to fire off their rifles. Especially at funerals—their specialty.

2. Hog Hogaboom was a mean dominoes
player and was owed money by most of the
guys down at the Hall. But he had a bunch
of ready cash in the bank from doing well in
the feed business. So he always said, "Pay
me the next time a train stops at the sta-
tion."

    Since the trains had not run through
town for twenty years and the tracks were
torn up as well, the losers were safe. Still,
a debt is a matter of pride. The VFW owed
him. Something. Sometime. Even more
than dominoes debts, they owed him for
paying for the stripper, who came once a
year between Thanksgiving and Christmas.

3. As with many couples who have been married for a long, long time, the Hogabooms'
marriage was a mix. Love and loathing. Respect and fear. Tolerance and disgust. Triumph and tragedy. Old Lady Hogaboom
(eighty-six) simply wanted to accompany
the casket to the cemetery, have it opened
one last time ("to make damn sure he's in
it," she said), and have a short service—the
less said, the better. She also wanted to
stay there until the casket was covered with
dirt.

    She was tired of him. And tired of herself.

And she also didn't know how she was going to go on without him. In the end, when the last shovel of earth was packed down, she wept when she turned away, and murmured, "I loved him."

She's buried there beside him now. Joined him less than six months later. But I am ahead of my story.

4. About fifty members of the Hogaboom clan gathered in the small town that week and hung around the porch of the grandparents' big old white frame house. Doing the relatives' dance. Making careful, quiet talk. Which was unusual since the Hogabooms were not noted for tranquillity; all hell usually broke out when they got together, but this was the death of a grandfather. For all his faults, most of them loved him. So they had spent a tense week—carrying unresolved feelings about their family around as carefully as they might handle hot coals. Wanting to leave now and wanting to stay forever at the same time. Wanting time to stand still and life to go on.

5. The VFW sent word via the mayor of the town asking please to be included in the funeral, and Old Lady Hogaboom pitched a fit that cleared the room. No, sir!, they were NOT coming under ANY circumstances. *No.* Period. She wouldn't have it.

6. So the VFW decided to hold a wake for Hog down at their hall the night before the funeral. And they hired the stripper one last time, in Hog's memory. It was the least they could do. Like I say, they owed him big.

Keep those program notes in mind as we come to Saturday morning, when the funeral procession wound its slow, solemn way out to the burying ground. A long, narrow cemetery. On a bluff above a runty little river. Grove of trees at one end. Freshly dug grave out in the middle of rows of worn tombstones. Faded canvas tent, plastic grass, folding chairs, two funeral directors—one old, one young. The usual. The family gathered, and the coffin was brought up from the hearse, carried by sons and grandsons. The widow was given her one last look before the lid was sealed and the coffin placed on straps to lower it into the earth. Quiet. Stillness. I opened my Bible to read the inevitable old words out of Ecclesiastes. "To everything there is a season, and a time for every purpose under heaven."

And a time for the Veterans of Foreign Wars. For at that moment, there came a blast of bugles and a roll of drums. Out of the trees at the far end of the cemetery marched the entire ambulatory membership of the local post of the VFW in ragged formation. Haphazard guys in haphazard uniforms. Hung over from the wake the night before. But with a fierce look in their eyes remembered from going over the tops of the trenches in France. They *owed* Hogaboom, by God. He had spent more time with them than he had with his wife and family. And, by God, they would pay him their last respects or else.

They halted. The drill sergeant shouted commands. The rifle team raised their white rifles and fired.

Looking back, I think the sheer shock of the sound of the first volley jarred something loose in the widow's mind. Or it just may have been that Old Lady Hogaboom noticed the VFW had brought the stripper with them.

She hollered, "NO, NO, NO!" She hiked up her dress, and swinging her purse over her head, she charged out across the cemetery calling the VFW names they didn't know women knew. She threatened to do to them what is prohibited by the Geneva Convention. As she stormed down upon them, the ranks of the veterans of war broke as they scrambled for cover off into the trees. Leaving rifles, bugles, drums, and flags behind. A total rout.

With deliberate dignity, Old Lady Hogaboom walked back toward those of us standing dumbfounded at the grave. She was smiling.

She had wanted to do that for years. Too bad her husband wasn't alive to see it. "Did you see that!" she shouted as she marched back toward us. "Did you see those old coots RUN? Chicken-hearted sonsabitches!"

The family broke up in laughter—at Grandma, themselves, the VFW, and the ludicrous turns this amazing life can take. Then Grandma cried and the family cried and I've told you what happened after that. William Lefhart Hogaboom II was laid to rest alongside his family, some of whom had gone on before him, and others who would come along behind him in time. Rest in peace.

When Old Lady Hogaboom passed away, I was not available to conduct the funeral. But I always wondered if the drum-and-bugle corps showed up for the occasion. I hope they did. Hogfart would have wanted it that way.

"Would you mind talking to my father about his tombstone?"

A request from a woman whose old dad was dying, and who was having a hard time dealing with her father's enthusiasm for planning every detail of the coming funeral and interment. The whole family was upset. Maybe someone a little more objective and a little more experienced with funerals could handle the morbid conversation.

The father indeed proved quite cheerful about the inevitable, and was a memorable short-term companion. His body was shot, but his mind was still lively, and he was determined to keep busy and be useful as long as breath remained. He had the service all worked out, the gravesite chosen and paid for. Even the shape and size of the simple granite tombstone had been determined.

It was his epitaph that concerned him. What he had in mind was a phrase that had truth in it—something he had often thought or said—something out of real life. Not too solemn, not too pretentious:

If only I could get through this week. . . .

He explained that he had said those words many times throughout his life. The phrase reflected his basic belief that life was tough, but, being an optimist, if he'd hang in there, things would get better. Realizing that this was not a particularly noble sentence, he wanted his final choice translated into Latin. To give the tombstone a little class. Just for fun. He was pleased with my amused cooperation.

A high school teacher of Latin did the work, but the old man died before I could get the translation back to him. The service he planned was accomplished as he wished. Included in the service was an observation he put down on paper the day he died:

I noticed a leaf on the ground this morning. Once it was lime green and now it's brilliant yellow. I wondered what it would be like if human beings fell off the tree of life in a blaze of colorful glory instead of just turning gray or going bald. It would be grand if fire would return one last time to face and hair. Why this drabness for human beings? As for me, if I had another week I'd have my hair dyed purple like those young people I see on the street. Purple is the color of ripeness and fruition, you know.

I wish we could have had his hair dyed purple for him—he deserved it, and what harm would it do? But his time ran out, and this time he didn't get through the week. His tombstone stands silent watch in the cemetery now. His name. Dates. And the words he wanted:

Utrum per hebdomadem perveniam.

The first funeral service I ever performed left a bad taste in my mouth. First year in the ministry. Twenty-four years old. Knew it all. No need to seek advice about anything. Which is why I so easily agreed to help a lady scatter the ashes of her husband from an airplane flying over Bellingham Bay. No problem. Go up in the plane. Open the door. Pour out the ashes. Say a few comforting words about death. Go home.

The pilot assumed I knew what I was doing. The widow assumed I knew what I was doing. And I was *certain* I knew what I was doing. So up we went. I even wore my brand-new black clerical gown for the occasion.

Over the middle of the bay, at about five thousand feet, the pilot held the cockpit door open, and I took the top off what looked like a two-quart ice-cream container and poured the ashes out the door.

The slipstream poured the ashes right back in the door.

Filling the cockpit with the final dust of Harry, the deceased husband.

Covering the widow, the pilot, and me.

The results of intensive cremation are kind of like flour. Clean flour, though. Purified by fire. Which is why you wouldn't be harmed if you happened to get a lot of it in your mouth and nose. As I did. Also the pilot. And the widow.

The conventions of behavior are not clear in these circumstances. You're not really sure if spitting or blowing your nose is respectful of the deceased.

We flew back to the field in silence.

There's not a lot to say at such times.

This situation was not covered in seminary training.

I can now add a practical paragraph to the *Ministers' Manual:* "If the ashes of the deceased are blown back into the cockpit, return to the airport and borrow a vacuum cleaner from the airport janitor and vacuum the deceased from the plane. NOTE: It is *very* important first to put a clean bag into the vacuum cleaner—something you may forget to do in your haste."

The widow was nice and calm and cool about the whole thing. "This will be . . . funny . . . someday," she said, and drove off alone in her own car with Harry's ashes beside her in the vacuum-cleaner bag.

I don't know what finally happened to Harry. I'm still too embarrassed to inquire. But I do wonder sometimes what else was with him in the bag and what happened when they poured Harry out the next time.

*W*hen I think about the words of "Rock-a-bye-baby," I'm amazed that we sing such a violent song to babies in the cradle. When I think about what I know now at age fifty-three, I guess it's just as well that children know from the beginning that pleasure and violence are neighbors. It's a long, old story.

It was spring and Easter week and all the eggs were broken. Dozens. In the street, on cars, fences, gates, a roof or two, and in every mailbox on our block it was the same. Broken eggs. Even more than broken—busted. Thrown hard. With malice and forethought. Sometime Friday evening, an attack had been made by persons unknown.

The eggors had made a special target of Mrs. Mooseker's house, cats, and her wimpy dog, Piggy (on account of his eating habits). Known in the neighborhood as "Old Miz Moose Eater," to assault the lady's domain was to kick the dragon's tail. And she, of course, was the first to get the news of the egging. Come Saturday morning, her two pussycats whipped in through the cat door coated with raw egg, setting off a red alert in the mind of their mistress. She charged right out the front door in her ancient purple satin robe with matching house slippers, and in her haste stepped in the middle of another mess of eggs that was located on Piggy, who was located up against the door, and whose oncoming hulk had sent the cats into the house in a hurry in the first place. Piggy howled, and Miz Moose Eater howled with him, seeing as the dog had sent her sprawling into yet another mess of broken eggs on the porch.

Old Miz Moose Eater rather enjoyed hysteria, and this was not an opportunity to be missed. So she uncorked a full-throated five-alarm bingo that alerted most of the neighborhood. "HELP, HELP, HELP, POLICE, POLICE, POLICE!" cried she. Then she went in to the phone and called the Fire Department.

Now unless one could lend credibility to a

theory that our neighborhood had been dive-bombed by an organized flock of irritated leg-horns, flying low and feeling fecund in unison, the answer to the Who? and the Why? of the Great Egg Attack would occur to any semi-calm person in the neighborhood pretty quick. If Old Miz Moose Eater was the eggee, then the identity of the eggors was clear. Seven small children between the ages of five and eight were in trouble.

You know the rest of the story. Most likely sometime in your life, as parent or child, you have been the reluctant guest at one of these neighborhood air-raid-and-cookouts.

After the alarm was spread, and I do mean the ALARM WAS SPREAD COMPLETELY, by Old Miz Moose Eater, who returned to her porch for another round of "HELP, HELP, POLICE," the neighborhood gathered. (You learn a lot about your neighbors under these conditions, because they do not turn up in their party clothes and makeup. It's a come-as-you-are event. A kind of instant Halloween-at-the-re-fugee-camp motif that would be amusing under other circumstances.)

The next act of this homely drama is called "The Rounding Up of the Usual Suspects." As you would guess, no children under age eight had turned up at the rally at Miz Moose Eater's house. Funny how kids always think that if they will just lie low and be cool, nobody will ever think they are the culprits. And funny how mothers always know. That's because mothers read minds. (Mothers also check refrigerators at times like this and count eggs—but a kid is too dumb to think of this.) And if it so happens there are about eight dozen eggs missing, then it is not going to be too long before four mothers and seven little kids are going to be gathered together. Along with Old Miz Moose Eater, a fire truck, and Piggy, the egg-coated dog, who was fiercely holding the firemen at bay.

A mom who tended to confuse motherhood with the Marine Corps led the inquisitional charge at the trial. And she ripped off that list of questions no kid in his right mind is even going to *try* to answer. "How did this happen?" Silence. "All right, then, who started it?" Many fingers point. "Why did you do this?" she demands of her own son. No kid has ever been able to answer that one, but every kid walks into the trap just the same and says, "I don't know," and then the Zen master sergeant retorts, "What do you mean you don't know?" And the kid walks right into the punch again with "I don't know what I mean that I don't know." And the mother volleys back, "Don't you talk back to me!" And the kid rises to the bait: "How come you ask me questions if you don't want me to answer?" And the mother slam-dunks it with "Don't you get smart with me or you'll *get IT* when I get you home." No kid wants IT, whatever IT is, so it's time for the kid to resort to penitential snorking—half sob and half hiccup. The kid does this so the mother will think she has broken his heart with her cruelty and will lay off. The kid also snorks because he realizes that he has somehow just confessed his guilt, and that's the last thing he meant to do.

Then comes the question that leads to neighborhood blood feuds: "Just exactly who did start this?" It is a lesser crime if a kid was corrupted by group pressure and somebody else's child is in fact the rotten apple in the barrel. Somehow it's OK if you were just blindly following the leader, but if you were the leader, you're in trouble. The testimony of the eggors is contradictory and confused, but it is clear none are innocent of the crime. No confessions. All are going down with the ship. Since it is part of the Children's Code that they will settle scores with each other after their mothers get through with them, the kids finally go mute in a gesture of group guilt. Better to be a criminal than a fink.

The Chief Judging Mother throws the book at them. The kids think they just tossed around a few eggs. But the judge declares them guilty of stealing, lying, vandalism, pollution, assault, and sin in the eyes of Almighty God. And what's more, if this ever happens again, they will spend the rest of their days in the children's ward of the state penitentiary. But for now they will, by God, clean up all this mess on their hands and knees with their tongues, apologize to all victims of the Great Egg Attack, and pay for the eggs out of their allowances, which will take FOREVER. "DO YOU UNDERSTAND?" Bowed heads nod. Sniveling and snorking is heard once more.

The condemned are led away. Old Miz Moose Eater smiles and goes home. The firemen have long gone. They were not smiling when they left.

You will note that no mention of fathers has been made. When the egg hit the fan, so to speak, the fathers found something that needed doing in backyards and basements. Fathers know when to lie low. Later they all wound up in one guy's garage drinking beer, petting dogs, and laughing their heads off

you start throwing a few eggs, you might as well throw all you've got—you can't just throw a few eggs, now, can you? No more than you can throw just a few snowballs or set off just a few of your firecrackers or have a well-controlled food fight. If everybody's doing it, how can you not join in? And once you start throwing eggs, it's amazing how many interesting targets there are and how quickly mischief turns to meanness and attacks on those who deserve it, like Old Miz Moose Eater and her dog, Piggy.

Does all this sound familiar?

Would it also sound familiar if I told you that's not the end of the story?

An ongoing topic of conversation among the kids was what was happening to Piggy underground. His was the first death and funeral in the neighborhood, and the children had kept his memory alive by telling each other ghoulish tales of the return of the dog from hell.

Five years later, on Halloween night, when it was known that Mrs. Moose was in San Diego visiting her niece, the same sinful seven—now between ten and thirteen years of age—decided to disinter old Piggy to see what shape he was in. With flashlights and shovels the juvenile archeologists went about the business of undigging Piggy. He had not been planted all that deep, but they must have forgotten just where, or else he was deeper than they thought, because quite a moat had been dug around the tree before a few bones turned up.

And the bones turned up just about the time Old Lady Moose Eater did. She had gone to the airport, all right, but to pick up her niece who was coming to visit from San Diego. The headlights from the car caught the culprits with bones in hand as she pulled into her driveway. Seven kids, a small moat around a tree, picks and shovels and the bones of Piggy, the Blessed One, in their hands. Grave robbers. Call 911.

And you can guess what happened after that. Police, Fire Department, Medic One, mothers, fathers, and so on and so forth. The full catastrophe. Sorry, in a way, that I missed it. But not really.

The bones of Saint Piggy were reburied. In a pet cemetery this time. Perpetual care. Gates locked at night.

Think that's the end of the story?

Oh, no. For one thing, the tree died—the one the kids dug the ditch around while looking for Piggy. Then the cats died—the ones Piggy chased in the house to set off the alarm in the first place. Miz Moose claimed the cats were poisoned—they don't usually kick off two at a time. And the usual suspects were rounded up once again. And so on.

Finally, the old lady herself died. Went to be with her Piggy and her tree and her cats.

End of story? Not yet. Of course not.

The reason I keep so up to date on all this is that one of the older kids in this endless soap opera works in the supermarket where I shop. His job: dairy department, stocking the egg section—a job he hates. He's always getting goo from broken eggs all over him. He figures Old Miz Moose Eater had the last laugh. He's getting married this summer. Wants to have kids. And the time will come, some Easter week, when the story will continue for him. This ritual morality play has no end.

There is violence in the world and in us. All of us. It will always be there to be confronted, as long as we are here to confront. When we are children, blindly following the urges of violence gets us in trouble with our moms. When we are adults, blindly following the urges of violence will get us all killed. Rock-a-bye-baby . . . and down will come baby, cradle, and all.

*J*ust above the light switch by the door to the studio where I work, I often place a photo-graph—pinning it to the wall with a red push-pin. When, in a magazine or a newspaper, I find a particularly arresting picture—a visual image that provokes my mind—I tear it out and put it by the light switch so that I see it and consider it as I come and go. Something to inspire me or confront me. For most of the month of March 1990, three photographs were pinned there by the light switch together.

A small one, in color, showed a middle-aged man doing some carpentry. Wearing aged leather hightop work shoes, blue jeans, flannel shirt, sweat-stained red baseball cap, and around his waist, a well-used nail apron. He is working about eight feet off the ground, straddling a wall header while he nails it to the corner post. He's framing a house, and by the look on his face and the way he holds the hammer, it is clear that he not only knows what he is doing, but is intent on doing it right and well. You see carpenters every day doing this common task—nailing wood to wood with hammer and nail and muscle and blood and sinew and brain. Men who say, when asked, "Well, I'm in construction work." I like looking at this picture—bright blue sky, new wood, an ancient trade—something very honest and positive going on.

The second picture by the light switch was a grainy black-and-white news photo from the morning paper earlier in the month. Showing a middle-aged man, in a short-sleeved, sweat-stained khaki shirt. The man is smiling a great smile. And the other people in the picture are also smiling. The occasion is the conclusion of an election—an honest election—held in powder-keg conditions in a Central American country. Nobody was killed during the elections, and the losers accepted the results, leading to a major change in government. The man in the shirtsleeves was there risking his credibility and brains and skills—even his life—to help bring about the impossible. He was there on his own, representing only himself and his concerns, without compensation other than the wages of conscience.

The third picture by the light switch shows a man in white shirt and tie. He is not smiling. The look on his face is a combination of vexation and determination. He has come once again to meetings in the Middle East to get enemies to talk to one another face to face. Not on behalf of his government or any government—not on behalf of any organization. On behalf of peace and justice. An agent of progress in human affairs.

It's the same man in each of these pictures by the light switch. And he is truly in the construction business. Giving of his time and life to build houses for poor people, to build an atmosphere wherein free elections can take place, to build structures of peace in one of the oldest and harshest arenas of conflict in human history.

The man's name is Carter. Used to raise peanuts in Georgia. Had a government job once. Carpenter now. And teacher. And when the historians settle up accounts on the twentieth century someday, his name will shine. He may not be in the list of great presidents—it is too soon to say. But it is not too soon to say that he is the finest ex-president in our century, and maybe ever.

Each night as I finished my work and paused at the switch, I looked at the three pictures. *Gallant* is the word that comes to mind—high-spirited, courageous. He knows how to lose—for he has lost big. Forces beyond his control may have made him the wrong man for the wrong job at the wrong time. Still, he lost as few men have.

He might have tucked his tail between his legs and spent the rest of his life sorting his papers and fishing and playing golf. Others who have had his government job have done as little. But *to lose* and *to be a loser* are very different matters. Besides, he still had work to do. Tasks he accepts because of who he is and not because of any office he may or may not hold. He is proof that there is no limit to the amount of good a man may do if he does not worry about who gets the credit.

He is not one of those who gained the whole world and lost his own soul.

His example is not lost upon me.

Thanks to that man.

To him, the noble prize.

One summer I worked on a ranch in Colorado as a horse wrangler, and lived in a bunkhouse with a cowboy named Gene who was a bona fide clockhead. We called him Mean Gene the Time Machine. ("Mean" is a compliment—used to describe a good cow horse or a new truck—as in "That there horse (or truck) is a *mean* piece of work.") Anyhow, Gene got the rest of his name because he could tell you the time—day or night—give or take five minutes, even though he never carried a watch. Mean Gene. He *always* knew what time it was. He didn't know just how he did it, but the rest of us figured he had a clock in his head that took up most of the room where his brain was supposed to be.

Mean Gene could set his head at night for whatever time he wanted to get up, and sure enough, dead on a bull's-eye, the next morning his eyelids would suddenly swing up like tiny garage doors in his head—you could almost hear the click and the whine of the little motors as Gene's mind opened for business for another day. Even when all the horse wranglers had been out dancing and carrying on until the small hours of the night and were looking at about three hours' sleep before breakfast, we could count on Gene. We'd fall into bed, and the foreman would turn off the light and say, "Gene, set your head," and Gene would ask, "Five or five-fifteen?" "Oh, five-fifteen'll do, Gene." "Right, g'night." We never missed a breakfast once.

Sometimes we took Mean Gene into town the weekend before payday and used him to win bar bets to buy beer. We'd put a blindfold on him and bet somebody that Gene could say when any number of minutes had gone by, and some fool would go for eleven minutes, say, and eleven minutes later old Gene would holler, "TIME FOR A BEER!" right on the money.

We thought we were in real trouble once when a hard-looking truck driver called for fifty-nine minutes. Now that's a long time to stand around a tavern waiting for a beer with nothing better to do than watch a guy in a blindfold think. Did he do it? Damn right he did! He *had* to. None of us had any money, and we would have had to buy beers for the truck driver and maybe ten of his friends if we had lost. Gene may have been a clockhead, but he wasn't *stupid.*

After that, Mean Gene the Time Machine became something of a local attraction on Friday nights. When he'd played the game long enough to set up about three beers apiece for us, he'd quit and go have a meatloaf-and-ketchup sandwich with some french fries, and head for the ranch. He didn't want to overdo a good thing.

Gene had talent. He had timing. He knew when to get off the stage and go home. A real professional clockhead, he was. And all the ranch hands were proud to be bunking with a guy in show business.

Unlike Gene, I've an irregular and ambivalent relationship with time. "An idiosyncratic periodicity" is the technical term that gives some dignity to my case. Keeping time is a useful social tool. I know that. But I would sure like to run a life that is not so time-bound. I try. I do try. In daily, practical terms this comes down to deciding to wear a watch or not.

My favorite watch—a compromise—is a handsome, serious-looking thing: gold case, black lizard strap—an antique. In the magazine ads, men wearing watches like this are suave, dignified, well-dressed, studly types, who exude wealth, breeding, and good taste. "Hunks" is what my daughter calls them. I do not appear to be a hunk. But then, my watch is not quite what it appears to be, either.

Up close you can see that this is an old-fashioned windup watch—its mechanical workings are all visible through the clear face. You can see the gears move and hear the soft ticking. Around the edge are the usual set of numbers. However. There are no hands on this watch.

The watch does not tell me what time it is.

It only tells me one thing—that the meter of my life is running and I should pay some attention to what I'm doing because each little turn of the wheel brings me closer to the end of my life.

The tick of this watch matches the pulse rate of my heart—sixty beats per minute. It's a *memento mori* ("remember death") watch—a perspective watch—that, in its own small way, tells my fortune.

And when asked the time, I look at my watch and reply, "I really can't tell."

Sometimes I just say, "Now."

. . .

On occasion I strap a small compass on my wrist instead of a watch. Gives me a fresh perspective on my daily routine around town, and prevents disorientation when on the road. The compass makes me substitute space for time as a dimension of life—think of sunrises instead of timetables, the location of stars instead of clocks, and the direction of weather instead of appointments.

And when asked, I can say, "Well, no, I don't know what time it is, but if you're lost, I can help you. Because I'm not." Met some fine people that way.

In my files is an advertisement for a watch that had me thinking hard for most of a week once. I was in my pocket-watch phase then, but not all my clothes had a proper pocket, so I was either going to have to get new pants or a new watch, and besides, a whole new generation of watches was being born. Digital. Quartz. Progress. Count me in.

The ad announced the Pulsar—"the first completely new way to tell time in 400 years." More than that, the ad copy proclaimed this watch the new international status symbol: the delight of emperors, celebrities, diplomats, senators, governors, and stars. It had fifteen hundred transistors, no moving parts, nothing to wear out or oil or maintain. Two thousand five hundred fifty times the force of gravity would not harm it. Waterproof, made of stainless steel that would not scratch or rust or mildew. It was run by a quartz crystal vibrating at 32,768 times a second. The face was lit by a tiny lamp built to last through more than a thousand years of regular use. It would keep time accurate to the millisecond per century.

I was impressed.

Just what I needed.

So I *almost* got one. For a week, I almost got one.

On reflection from some years away from the moment of decision, I think that watch alienated me. For all its admirable technology, it set standards much higher than I was comfortable being close to. The watch was too good for me.

So I kept the pocket watch. We have a compatible relationship.

It's unreliable and unpredictable—like me. We both require attention and affection and patience to keep us working well. The watch is easily affected by heat and pressure. Like me. Neither one of us is waterproof or works well below freezing. My watch runs down, and is rusting and corroding and wearing thin in places. Sometimes it doesn't work at all. Me, too.

My old pocket watch won't last a thousand years. But it gets me by one day at a time, and is reasonably accurate about what it has to tell. You could say the same about me.

I still have it and use it when I wear those old-fashioned pants with the built-in pockets. The pants with pleats and suspender buttons and linings at the knees. I notice the pants are back in fashion. Maybe pocket watches are next.

Instead of being thought of as a regressive old coot who still wears wide ties and doesn't have a decent watch, a guy like me would be there in the ads with the pretty girls and expensive cars and fine wines—wearing his pocket watch—there on the shores of Lake Como in the summer afternoon. Laid-back, smiling. Like we had all the time in the world.

A question with several possible answers comes to mind: If one man lives as though he would never die and another man lives as though he might die tomorrow, would either one wear a wristwatch?

When I get to thinking about time, I always wonder what happened to Mean Gene the Time Machine. As I write this, it's thirty years later. Maybe he did what the ranch foreman suggested and got himself a career as a human time clock in a factory. I imagine him sitting there by the door in the sunshine, and guys walking through the door saying their names and slapping him a high five. Probably not. Gene wasn't too good at remembering names.

See, the Law of Compensation applied to Gene. His time powers were offset by the generally disorderly function of the rest of his brain. He was forever losing things, never got compass directions right, and couldn't remember the names of the horses from one day to the next. Absentminded. Or maybe he was just presentminded somewhere else.

Why this obsession with time? Why is it strapped so tightly around our wrists and minds? Will we ever have enough time? What would happen if we only had enough time? When will the time finally come? Who knows where the time goes? How far is it from time to time? What time is the right time? Will we know when our time has finally come? These are not questions addressed by reason, I think. Though at least a part of an answer may be found in a story I heard in a café in Nebraska.

(Mean Gene, this one's for you.)

Seems a man is riding along in the country

and he sees a far̥
air under a tree. Th
takes a closer look.
pig up to eat an apple,
one, the farmer move.
under another apple. Nc
pig, and the farmer is strḁ
buckets—but still patiently
this unusual way, apple afte

So the traveler goes over t̥
says, "That's a strange way
Doesn't it take a lot of time?"

"Sure does," replies the farmei
time to a pig?"

*T*he electric power is out at our house today. We knew it was going to happen. Also, the water is off. We knew about that, too. A woman wearing a hard hat hung a little pink card on our front doorknob yesterday. Explaining, in special public-utility language designed to cover all possible bases and reveal very little, that our power would be off at midnight for several hours. This is happening on the same day the plumber fixed some PVC pipe in the bathroom with glue that takes twenty-four hours to dry. So here we are. Nice fall weather. Clear skies. No disaster, no panic, no excitement. Also no electricity or water. Time for candles and a bucket. The simple life. Strange feeling, this. Like a taste of the end of life as we know it. Hard to believe that for most of the world, this is still life as they know it. And was the way of life for most people in this country until almost World War II. In fact, up until about 1700, the only power available anywhere in any form came from wind, running water, animals, or human muscle.

My father, born in 1900, grew up this way.

The only power under his command was his own and the horse he rode.

And now, just one generation later, his son is up to his wazoo in power. Over lunch I started making a list of all the motors I own—all the power at my command. Motors in three clocks, a stereo (three motors), the washer, the dryer, vacuum cleaner, portable heater with fan, overhead fan, coffee grinder, mixer, toaster, oven, microwave, refrigerator, juicer, blender, sewing machine, two hair dryers, my wife's Water Pik, one inboard diesel motor in the sailboat, one outboard motor for the dinghy, one automobile engine, submotors in the car to raise and lower and blow one thing and another, one truck engine, one motorcycle engine, two watch mechanisms, and some windup toys. Moreover, there are all those power-driven hand tools in the shop—drill, screwdriver, portable saw. And that's just at home. Just counting the ones that are known to work. Never mind the ones that don't work anymore and will never work again but are kept around because I am going to fix them someday. At the office there's the fax machine and the copy machine, plus computers and printers, telephones, a heater, and an electric pencil sharpener that works sometimes. I'm sure I've missed some. Motors. Electric and gas. All this power. Mine.

The ridiculous thing—the *really* ridiculous thing—is that I haven't a clue as to how any of these motors work or how to fix them if they don't work. No problem. If it breaks, just buy a new one, right? Not because they can't be fixed—that's an excuse—but because I don't want to admit how stupid or lazy or helpless or busy I am. I buy new ones so nobody knows about my inadequacies but me. I can live with knowing I'm stupid, but not with other people knowing. This is why we have a whole lot of hardware stores. So men don't have to feel stupid in public. This is not a sexist remark. My wife can fix things. Male pride is a burden.

I have a scheme for a new business—a repair shop. Run like the way the Catholic Church used to run confessionals. You go into a big dark building that looks like a church and you go into a small booth that has a privacy screen on it so nobody can see who you are and you tell whoever is on the other side of the screen that your toaster is dead and you can't fix it, and then you slip it through a slot in the wall with a twenty-dollar bill. The person behind the screen absolves you of your stupidity by saying that it's OK—a person of your caliber and dignity has more important things to do. A week later, your toaster is delivered by mail, addressed to "postal patron." This is called an exercise in power—the power of mind over matter. If you don't mind being inadequate, it doesn't matter.

Someone was telling me about a game of imagination wherein you can go back to any time in history and all you can take with you is your knowledge and experience and skills. No tools or equipment or books. You are to pick a time and place and event wherein your intervention will make a difference to the outcome of history or make you rich. Your credibility will be based on your capacity to deliver proof of your capacities. Easy. Well, not so easy. Just because you know history and will seem to be able to foresee the future doesn't mean anybody will believe you, for one thing. They all thought they knew what they were doing at the time. Custer wouldn't have listened to you. So go way back in time before guns. The Romans might be interested in what you know about guns. But can you make one? Can you come up with tempered steel, gunpowder? Well, okay, some other time in history—you know about telephones, right? Just because you can take a toaster apart doesn't mean you know anything about electricity or anything powered by electricity, especially how telephones work. What do you really know how to do and make? Jell-O. You know how to make Jell-O. Where does the stuff Jell-O is made from come from? Some part of a cow's foot, you've heard. Which part, and how do you get it from there into the Pyrex bowl and the refrigerator, which you don't know how to make, either? Never mind. Fire. How about fire? Where do you get flint and steel? Ever made a fire with flint and steel? Want to feel really stupid in public? Do history a favor and stay here.

My friend Willy is a serious fan of wonder-and-awe. Not cosmic wonder-and-awe, just ordinary, underfoot wonder-and-awe. We go running together every Monday, Wednesday, and Friday. He keeps me in touch with golf, baseball, medicine, and fathering small children—all of which I am either not into or already out of. We're friends in no small part because he is one of the few people I can talk to about things like how many motors I own, and also because he can usually come up with something in the same class of deep human concern. This morning I shared my meditation on motors and power with him. He came back with balls.

He had noticed an accumulation of balls in the trunk of his car. A baseball, couple of golf balls, soccer ball, football, two marbles, plastic beachball (dead), a squash ball, a can of tennis balls, and a bowling ball. In his garage are balls for croquet. In his house he found Ping-Pong balls, a Wiffle ball, basketball, several ball bearings of unknown origin, a set of juggling balls, and five sizes of all-purpose play balls in the children's rooms. And in his music collection, a recording of Jerry Lee Lewis singing "Great Balls of Fire."

Round things. All his. Millions of active young American fathers must have a similar collection. This is democracy, the American Way, progress, plenty, and capitalism—the high-water mark of human history. All the balls you want. Cheap.

We ran about six blocks in silence considering this abundance of power and balls.

Then I asked him the what-if-you-went-back-in-history question.

No problem. Willy would go way, way back. Before balls and ball games. He'd teach people games to play with balls. He thinks it would change history.

"But, Willy, you don't know how to make perfectly round objects or the materials used or pumps to blow them up."

"No problem. Rocks. Pig bladders. Cow udders. Coconuts. Oranges. Melons."

"But, Willy, none of those are perfectly round."

"Well, we might have to change the rules a little at first, but it can be handled. More and better ball games earlier on would have changed history. If Moses had come down off the mountain with a set of golf clubs and a few round rocks instead of the Ten Commandments, the children of Israel would have had a better time. And I can't imagine Columbus leaving town when the World Series was on. Or what would have happened if Columbus had been met by the real Washington Redskins ready to play any Sunday he was ready? Never mind the turkey and pie, let's play some ball."

As a parting gift when he was going out of the country for a sabbatical year to be a doctor in New Zealand, I gave Willy the ultimate Swiss

Army knife. Fourteen blades, some with multiple functions—pliers, scissors, a saw, magnifying glass, fish scale, can opener, three screwdrivers, an awl, a punch, a chisel, and two cutting blades. Plus detachable tweezers, ballpoint pen, and toothpick. The knife came in a black leather case to wear on your belt. And that case had little compartments that contained a compass, safety pin, piece of string, a Band-Aid, piece of paper, two waterproof matches, a quarter, and two aspirin. Awesome. Willy asked me if he had to have a license to carry the thing around with him. Most people would have seen the gift as a portable tool kit to use to try to fix things with when the real tools weren't handy. Not Willy.

For him it was a tool of the imagination. Each and every feature of the Swiss Army knife became the centerpiece of an adventure story of the amazing Roger Dodger, a ten-year-old boy whose ordinary life was turned into great adventure by the Swiss Army knife. He fell down a laundry chute one day into the Diamond Kingdom. Willy told the tale of peril and triumph to his two young children while traveling through New Zealand and Australia. In each episode, the hero used one of the parts of the Swiss Army knife kit to escape from danger and elude his evil pursuers. The surroundings of the moment wherever they happened to be traveling was the background of each story. Sometimes a story took days as Willy set his fairy-tale fishing hook deep in the minds of his children and reeled them around and around the great lake of mysterious adventure. His children will never forget the trip. One look at a Swiss Army knife and it all comes back.

This Swiss Army thing intrigues me. Maybe it's because we can identify with an army that never goes to war and never takes sides and minds its own business. There's something civilized about a GI knife that includes a corkscrew to open wine bottles with. A Swiss Army watch is on the market now, and a Swiss Army parka on the way.

I'm told Tiffany's sells a sterling silver and 18-karat gold version of the standard Swiss Army penknife.

My friend Willy and I were running along one morning and got to speculating on how we might get in on the Swiss Army mania. We came up with Swiss Army underpants for men. Black, so they won't get dyed pink in the home wash, something that has happened to the white briefs belonging to both of us. Besides, black is sexy and macho, something Willy and

I aspire to be, especially if all we had to do was wear the right shorts. The Swiss Army underpants would have to have a red-and-white trim stripe around the top and legs so that you could whip off your trousers to go swimming and people would think you had on a bathing suit. This is in the Swiss Army tradition of multiple uses for an item. Also in the Swiss Army tradition is durability. Stainless steel is a little heavy for underpants, so ours would be woven of ballistic-quality nylon for strength, cashmere wool for warmth, and silk for sexiness. There would be an inner lining of reflective Mylar so you could use your underpants as a solar cooker or to reflect light to signal for help if you were stranded.

Inside the waistband, we'd sew some emergency information. Like the order of what beats what in a poker game. Because most guys can't remember if a flush beats a straight and which one of those beats three-of-a-kind. This way you could just check your drawers and you'd know and wouldn't look stupid for thinking you won but didn't.

Most guys could use a place in the waistband of their underpants to write their Social Security number on, and maybe their car license, and their office fax number. There ought to be room to write in their wedding anniversary and a few birthdays.

And these Swiss Army underpants ought to look so good and be so indestructible that a man would never ever have to worry about his mother's warning to always wear clean underwear in case he was in an accident and had to go to the emergency room at the hospital. The doctors would start cutting your clothes off you, and someone would say, "Wow, this guy's wearing Swiss Army underpants!" Nothing but the best of care for you.

My friend Willy reminds me of a juggler who came to our church one Christmas Eve for the midnight service. I wanted to read an old story from long ago about a wandering juggler who happened into a monastery in deep winter and asked for refuge. You may know this story. If memory serves me well, I think it's a French tale called "Our Lady's Juggler."

The story says that the monks were busy making gifts to lay before the high altar of the monastery chapel in honor of the Virgin Mary. Because if she was pleased, her statue would shed a tear of compassion for humanity. But when the gifts were presented at the Feast of the Nativity, the statue did not respond. In the middle of the night, the juggler, who thought he had no gift to give, went in alone and juggled before the statue—and juggled to the very limit of his capacity. To make a long story short, the statue of the Virgin Mary shed a tear—and the baby Jesus in her arms smiled—because the juggler had given everything he had, holding back nothing in his generosity. So goes the story.

To bring the story to life, I wanted to have a real juggler perform for the congregation first, and then I'd tell the story and turn it into my Christmas sermon. A little show-business pizzazz for the midnight service.

When time for the service came, the juggler had not arrived. Not until the middle of the second carol did I see him working his way up the crowded side aisle. But no costume. I had specifically asked him to wear his jester outfit. And no juggling equipment, either. What a disappointment. So much for magic at midnight.

While the congregation headed into the last verse of "O Little Town of Bethlehem," the juggler and I held a whispered conference. His car had been stolen, with all his possessions and equipment. But not to worry. A friend had brought him and would take him home afterward. In the meantime, he had an idea. All I had to do was tell the fairy story, and he, the juggler, would take it from there.

No time to argue. The carol was done, and the service had to go on. I assumed that when it came time for his performance, the juggler would explain his circumstances and use some things he had found in the church kitchen for a short act. Reasonable enough. However, Christmas Eve is not a time for reasonableness. I ought to know that by now.

So I read the story.

And the juggler stepped into the light from out of the congregation. Slim young man, the wiry, athletic kind. Black tennis shoes, jeans, green turtleneck shirt. Solemn expression and freckles on his face in place of the expected makeup. Longish brown hair. Nothing special to look at. And no tools of his trade.

He smiled. And began his routine. In fact, he went through his entire routine just as if he had brought balls and clubs and knives and scarves with him. We had all seen enough juggling to know what was going on. And in each part of the routine, he went one step further than he had ever juggled and we had ever seen. Seven balls is supposed to be the limit for the very best professional juggler. Our guy did eight, and we knew it when he did it and applauded the moment of triumph. On through twelve silk scarves in the air at once and seven knives, and we even knew when he set his torches on fire and got eight torches in the air all at once and caught them without

burning himself. We laughed and shouted en-
couragement and applauded this remarkable
performance. We couldn't see it, but we believed it. We gave him a standing ovation. On
Christmas Eve in church—a standing ovation.
He held up his hand for silence, and the congregation sat down. The juggler wasn't
through. He was going to do an encore.

He started juggling things we couldn't quite
recognize. What's this? Chickens? Birds?
Some kind of tree. Rings. One off of each
finger. Five? Five gold rings. Got it! "The
Twelve Days of Christmas." He was going to
juggle one of everything in the Twelve Days.
The partridge, the pear tree, and all the rest.
Impossible. But he was doing it. A swan. A
goose and an egg. I was thinking, He will never
get the maid and the cow off the ground, but
with a great heaving effort, he did it. After that,
the leaping lady and the dancing lord and the
drum with drummer were a piece of cake.
Every gift was in the air—way, way up in the
air, because this was a lot of stuff. And as each
piece came around, we knew what it was and
shouted out its name as he caught it and threw
it back into the air again. Fantastic! Nobody
had ever done this before. The juggler was
laughing. The congregation cheered like a
crowd at a championship game when a last-
minute score won it for the home team. The

juggler suddenly clapped his hands loudly and stood still. One finger in front of his lips called for silence. And silence came.

We stood looking at him and he at us. In the most powerful and meaningful moment of quiet I've witnessed at Christmas Eve. The sermon was supposed to follow the juggler. And it did. But it was not I who spoke. We were all addressed by a sermon of eloquent instructive silence. The silence in which we absorbed the power of the vision we had of the impossible event we had wished into being. The silence in which we thought about our capacity to realize things we can sometimes only imagine. Some of the most wonderful things have to be believed to be seen. Like flying reindeer and angels. Like peace on earth, goodwill, hope, and joy. Real because they can be imagined into being. Christmas is not a date on a calendar but a state of mind.

Someone—I don't know who—began to sing "Silent Night." As was our tradition, people on the first row lit their small candles from the big candle on the altar, and then passed the flame on to the candles of those in rows behind them. The church filled with light. And we filed out of the church singing into the night and went home, taking our light with us.

Over the last couple of years I have been a frequent guest in schools; most often invited by kindergartens and colleges. The environments differ only in scale. In the beginners' classroom and on university campuses the same opportunities and facilities exist. Tools for reading and writing are there—words and numbers; areas devoted to scientific experiment—labs and work boxes; and those things necessary for the arts—paint, music, costumes, room to dance—likewise present and available. In kindergarten, however, the resources are in one room, with access for all. In college, the resources are in separate buildings, with limited availability. But the most ap-

237

parent difference is in the self-image of the students.

Ask a kindergarten class, "How many of you can draw?" and all hands shoot up. Yes, of course we can draw—all of us. What can you draw? Anything! How about a dog eating a fire truck in a jungle? Sure! How big you want it?

How many of you can sing? All hands. Of course we sing! What can you sing? Anything! What if you don't know the words? No problem, we make them up. Let's sing! Now? Why not!

How many of you dance? Unanimous again. What kind of music do you like to dance to? Any kind! Let's dance! Now? Sure, why not?

Do you like to act in plays? Yes! Do you play musical instruments? Yes! Do you write poetry? Yes! Can you read and write and count? Yes! We're learning that stuff now.

Their answer is Yes! Over and over again, Yes! The children are confident in spirit, infinite in resources, and eager to learn. Everything is still possible.

Try those same questions on a college audience. A small percentage of the students will raise their hands when asked if they draw or dance or sing or paint or act or play an instrument. Not infrequently, those who do raise their hands will want to qualify their response with their limitations: "I only play piano, I only draw horses, I only dance to rock and roll, I only sing in the shower."

When asked why the limitations, college students answer they do not have talent, are not majoring in the subject, or have not done any of these things since about third grade, or worse, that they are embarrassed for others to see them sing or dance or act. You can imagine the response to the same questions asked of an older audience. The answer: No, none of the above.

What went wrong between kindergarten and college?

What happened to YES! of course I can?

On the occasion of his graduation from engineering college last June (*cum laude,* thank you very much), I gave my number-two son a gift of a "possibles bag."

The frontiersmen who first entered the American West were a long way from the resources of civilization for long periods of time. No matter what gear and supplies they started out with, they knew that sooner or later these would run out and they would have to rely on essentials.

These essentials they called their "possibles"—with these items they could survive, even prevail, against all odds. In a small leather bag strung around their neck they carried a brass case containing flint and steel and tinder to make fire. A knife on their belt, powder and shot, and a gun completed their possibles.

Many survived even when all these items were lost or stolen.

Because their real possibles were contained in a skin bag carried just behind their eyeballs. The lore of the wilderness won by experience, imagination, courage, dreams, and self-confidence. These were the essentials that armed them when all else failed.

I gave my son a replica of the frontiersmen's possibles bag to remind him of this attitude. In a sheepskin sack I placed flint and steel and tinder, that he might make his own fire when necessary; a Swiss Army knife—the biggest one with the most tools; a small lacquer box that contained a wishbone I saved from a Thanksgiving turkey—for luck; a small velvet pouch containing a tiny bronze statue of Buddha; a Cuban cigar in an aluminum tube; and a miniature bottle of Wild Turkey whiskey in case he wants to bite a snake or vice versa. Invisible in the possibles bag were his father's hopes and his father's blessing. The idea of

gathering quiet of oncoming night, he looks out at the people of this little town.

"Somewhere more than three hundred miles above the earth tonight, a telescope is in orbit. Put there because we want to know more. Put there because we want to see as far out there as we can see. Put there—well, just because. Like the eensy-weensy spider who went up the drainpipe in the song of childhood, we go out and up to know, again.

"Where we sit at the moment was once fire. All of it. The whole earth was molten rock. Life could not possibly happen here. But it did.

"Where we sit at the moment was once water. Thousands of feet of water covered this very place. And then salt—hundreds of feet. And then sand—thousands of feet. And then where we sit was lifted up and worn down and lifted up and worn down again and again. Carved by water and the same wind and dust that blew all day today.

"Someday the dust will cover this place again, and then water, and someday fire again, and someday, nothing.

"For a while, there were reptiles here as big as diesel locomotives. We take the schoolchildren to see their tracks, which are close by. Only the tracks and bones remain.

"And there were people in this very place,

long before. We call them Neanderthal and
Cro-Magnon, Basket-makers and Anasazi,
Utes and Spaniards. They called themselves
'the People Who Live Here.' As we do now.
We dig through the ruins of their homes and
wonder where they came from and where they
went and why. A long time from now, perhaps
other people will come and dig through our
ruins and wonder where we came from and
where we went and why we lived as we do.

"In this audience it is likely there is someone
pregnant with child unborn. In this audience
there are those who do not have long to live.
Somewhere out there are those who will marry
the members of the class of 1990—somewhere their homes . . . somewhere their children . . . somewhere their graves. Out there.
Somewhere.

"And in between now and then, the need to
eat, sleep, be dry and warm, to love and be
loved. In between now and then the same
struggle of Adam and Eve, east of our own
Edens. Good, evil, joy, sorrow, pain, promise,
light, darkness, poems, and wonder. *Star
Wars, Indiana Jones, The Hobbit,* 'Little Red
Riding Hood,' *Macbeth,* Wagner's *Ring,* the
eensy-weensy spider, and the story of the
people of this little town of Moab, Utah."

Suddenly there is a commotion off to my

right. Uh-oh. Two young men ringing cowbells, wearing cowboy boots, cowboy hats, face masks, and absolutely nothing else, plunge out of the darkness, flash across the lighted stage, and out into the night again, *clanging, clanging.* We have been streaked! Buck-naked youth has torn a hole in the fabric of solemnity. The audience shouts, whistles, laughs, applauds. I offer to have the streakers run by again in case anybody missed them the first time. The superintendent of schools tries gamely to supress his smile but cannot.

Once again the wild, young, green, foolish, mad, mischievous mystery of the unpredict-able has shot through our lives, energizing the moment with joy. Once again we have been caught by surprise.

At times like this we always say, "Well, you never know what's coming next."

The speaker knows enough to fold his cards here, for he and the streakers have about cov-ered (or uncovered) all that's essential for now. Long after the remarks of the speaker are forgotten, the streakers will be remem-bered. It's just as well. Surprise is at the core of existence. It's true. You never ever really know what's coming next.

The beat of the big bass drum begins anew. The band plays, the seniors walk by one by

one as their names are called, and on down
the aisle into the rest of their lives, followed by
family and friends and time into the night. They
know what they know. And know, somehow,
they still have a lot to learn.

The lights go out on the stage. The wind has
picked up again. The river rolls on.
    We are not the stony, dry ground over which
the wind blows and the rivers run. We are part
of that energy that gives the wind motion and
drives the river to the sea. From way out in
space, we shine—a lovely blue point of light in
the universe. Twinkle, twinkle, little star . . .

On the last page of *All I Really Need to Know I Learned in Kindergarten,* I promised to return and tell about "frogs; Miss Emily Phipps; a sign in a grocery store in Pocatello, Idaho; the most disastrous wedding of all time; a Greek phrase, *asbestos gelos* (unquenchable laughter); the Salvation Navy; the man who knew then what he knows now; the smallest circus in the world; the truth about high school; and the time when the bed was on fire when I lay down on it." By now, in one way or another, in this book and in the book *It Was on Fire When I Lay Down on It,* I have kept my word. Except for telling you about Miss Emily Phipps. I've been putting this off because while it's an important story, the telling may be a bit confusing. But a promise is a promise.

Emily Phipps worked for me part time for about two years. Before that, she was employed by a teaching colleague. Being a social secretary to the rich and famous was her profession. And since neither he nor I were rich and famous while Emily Phipps was in our employ, I shall explain.

For a number of years, at the end of the school year at our college-prep high school, the aforementioned colleague hosted a festive croquet party for his fellow teachers. The red-brick Georgian architecture of the school and its acres of green playing fields made an idyllic setting for this event, which became a parody of upper-class afternoon tea parties à la Oxford, Eton, and the rest. The dons and their women at play. A lawn party. A little sherry, some cheese, and sporting costume for the gentlemen were the order of the day. Parasols and long dresses for the ladies were expected. Though beer, tortilla chips, and cut-offs tended to be preferred by those who could not overcome their plebeian roots, an atmosphere of dignified good taste usually prevailed.

The invitations to this ruly (as opposed to

unruly) event were signed in elegant Victorian script by "Emily Phipps (Miss), social secretary." It was she who set the tone of the invitation with her inevitable sense of good manners, breeding, and taste. Her language was impeccable, and the subtlety of her innuendo as to what was and was not done was unimpeachable. Emily Phipps was admired by all, and my colleague was envied for the quality and devotion of his employee.

One year I asked if he would mind if Emily Phipps came to work for me for a while. Gracious man that he is, he so allowed.

At this time I was in the early stages of negotiations with people in the world of books back East in New York. An agent, an editor, and various other employees of the publishing company, including its president. It simply would not do not to have a secretary if I was to play in such a league.

A secretary may bring a certain objective and graceful voice to correspondence. A touch of class. A secretary may say things about her employer he may not say about himself, and may do things on the employer's behalf that he himself would not do. A secretary can provide reasons and excuses. A secretary can send cookies and flowers, and write thank-you notes. She heads an embassy in the diplomatic corps of business transactions. A secretary has great power in her hands, and frequently knows better how to use it than her boss.

Therefore it was quite clear that a man in my position needed an administrative assistant of the caliber of Emily Phipps (Miss).

Emily offered special assets—she worked cheap, was on call twenty-four hours a day, was never anything but easygoing and cheerful, required no Social Security or health-benefit payments, and never took paid vacations. A dream.

And also a figment of imagination.

You see, Emily Phipps, as you probably have guessed by now, did not really exist.

A fiction—the product of the inventive mind of my colleague and my own sense of mischief. We made her up and played her part.

Little did I imagine how real she was to become.

In the beginning, Emily Phipps did all the gracious and helpful things necessary to getting business relationships off to a good start. She sent cookies and flowers, wrote helpful letters with informative asides about her current employer, Mr. Fulghum, and took care of small details with efficiency. An older, wiser person than her boss, she knew his weaknesses, eccentricities, and habits. Her letters reflected a caring cynicism about his talents and skills. She was protective—not wanting him to get in over his head or lose the good life he had by plunging headlong into fame and fortune.

The people in New York liked Emily Phipps, and began writing letters to her instead of me, finding her easier to deal with than me. They sent her gifts, Christmas cards, and asked special favors of her.

I began to get letters of inquiry about Emily—"What does she look like, and how old is she, and what's she like in person?" "She's such a lovely woman—you're lucky to have her; not many people have an assistant who is both so loyal and so perceptive."

I remember well the moment when I realized that this whole thing had got out of hand and that I either had to confess the sham or carefully move Emily offstage and out of the play.

But it wasn't mischief anymore. Emily had become a part of me. An alter ego. A mirror that I held up and saw other dimensions of myself in. By keeping Emily alive and well and functioning, I kept looking at myself with new perspective. Emily Phipps taught me something new about me. I liked her, too. I needed what she was. She was a better person than I usually managed to be.

. . .

As an only child living some distance from the nearest neighbors, I had numerous imaginary playmates to keep me company. But I wasn't sure an adult could pull this off and still claim mental health. Or perhaps this is how playwrights think?

Nevertheless, Emily continued to work for me. Part time, of course. Until my literary agent, whom I had never met in person, decided to come from New York to Seattle for a visit. She especially was looking forward to meeting Emily. Uh-oh.

It just so happened that Emily had reached her sixty-fifth birthday that spring, and she decided to retire. Soon. Before my agent arrived. Emily bought five different pantsuits and set off with a friend in an Airstream trailer to see America. She would not be here to meet my agent.

But I had a real part-time secretary by then, and she had been let in on the Emily story and had even written some letters for Emily. This real secretary, Martha, was eighteen years old and headed for college in the fall. She could not play the part of Emily in person. There was nothing else to do but for Martha to become the niece of Emily Phipps, Edith Phipps. Martha would have to make a lot of smoke if this by-now totally ridiculous plot was to be played out. Martha was game. Martha could make a lot of smoke when she had to. My wife wanted no part of this deal, however, and thought about being out of town herself if Martha and I were going through with the charade.

And we pulled it off. Or thought we did.

To this day, I do not know how the beans were spilled. But I do know that when my agent returned home, she wrote saying that Emily Phipps had dropped in for coffee in New York and looked smashing in her new mango-orange pantsuit. The letter went on to say how wonderful a person she was and how grand it was for me to have her work for me for all these years. She liked Emily a great deal, especially in person.

I was nonplussed. Then delighted. To her everlasting credit, my agent had joined the plot instead of blowing the whistle on it. She must have made co-conspirators out of my editor and others in the publishing business touched by Emily. I do not know. We've never discussed it. Never will, I hope. A piece of great fun would be lost if we did. So Emily Phipps lives on as part of the drama we choose to make of our lives. Emily Phipps still works for me when she is in town. She is here this week, as a matter of fact. My agent and editor occa-

sionally speak of her. Somewhere in the land-
scape of our minds, Emily is still traveling—
seeing America. She occasionally drops in on
her niece, Edith, at Stanford. And still sends
cookies and flowers to people she admires.
Once in a while she writes a letter to the people back East, usually because she just happens to be in Seattle and just happens to be
filling in for my real assistant for a few days
and just happens to be good at straightening
out little glitches in personal and business
matters. Emily Phipps (Miss), has become real
and will always be real because those who
know her wish her existence to continue, and
are content that she be just who she is. As I
finish this, Emily is reading it over my shoulder.
The new pantsuit is yellow. Emily sends her
regards to you.

That's the truth.

What is the truth about any one of us? I often
wonder about that.

Psychiatrists, biographers, juries—even
close relatives—know how elusive it is.

The eye that looks in on us and the eye that
looks out from us is not the same eye.

Most of us create ourselves—arrange the
facts of our lives like flowers in a bowl—cutting
here, bending there, covering here, revealing

there, and filling in the blank spaces with greenery as needed. Everything we can imagine becomes real.

Fabulists. A word to put the best face on what we do. Fabulists. Tellers of tales.

Actors in many sit-coms across the time of our lives. Always the star in our show.

How shall we answer the question "Did you make all that up or is it true?"

With this reply: "Yes and no and I'm not sure sometimes myself."

I bought a stew bowl this past winter, and it sits before me now as I write. It's slightly larger than what you might ordinarily eat your morning cereal from. Made by hand, using clay dug from a canyon wash in New Mexico. After shaping and drying, the bowl was painted with a simple curving design representing the four winds, then fired outdoors in a pit, using dry chips of horse and cow manure for fuel. Finally, the bowl was polished with a bone, making it shine. The colors are rust, white, black, and red. The technique and design distinguish the bowl as a fine example of the ritual art of a Native American potter from the Pueblo culture of the Southwest. The bowl is a pleasure

to see and hold. It is meant to be used daily. Its maker told me that only half the bowls she begins survive the firing and polishing. And they are not forever—bowls break sooner or later. The bowl's existence and use depend upon the unpredictable variables of earth, water, fire, imagination, and luck. As does the existence of its user. (Potters understand about "uh-oh.") Nevertheless, she makes each bowl as well as she can, intending that it hold food and beauty equally well as long as it lasts. My stew bowl speaks to me. I like the values it embodies.

If you look closely at the design and follow it as it circles the rim of the bowl, you will notice a peculiar discontinuity. There is a small break—a ceremonial break, actually. The potters call this a "pathway." For a thousand years this line break has appeared in Pueblo pottery. It is there to indicate that while this particular vessel is finished, the life of the potter is not. It is a ritual sign of continuing possibility.

For the same reasons and in the same spirit, this book, this stew bowl of thought, ends with a semicolon;

Robert Fulghum, February 14, 1991

ROBERT FULGHUM is the author of *All I Really Need to Know I Learned in Kindergarten* and *It Was on Fire When I Lay Down on It.*